Lecture Notes
in Business Information Processing
404

Series Editors

Wil van der Aalst ⓘ
RWTH Aachen University, Aachen, Germany

John Mylopoulos ⓘ
University of Trento, Trento, Italy

Michael Rosemann ⓘ
Queensland University of Technology, Brisbane, QLD, Australia

Michael J. Shaw
University of Illinois, Urbana-Champaign, IL, USA

Clemens Szyperski
Microsoft Research, Redmond, WA, USA

More information about this series at http://www.springer.com/series/7911

Dietmar Winkler · Stefan Biffl ·
Daniel Mendez · Manuel Wimmer ·
Johannes Bergsmann (Eds.)

Software Quality

Future Perspectives on Software Engineering Quality

13th International Conference, SWQD 2021
Vienna, Austria, January 19–21, 2021
Proceedings

 Springer

Editors
Dietmar Winkler (ID)
TU Wien
Vienna, Austria

Stefan Biffl (ID)
TU Wien
Vienna, Austria

Daniel Mendez (ID)
Blekinge Institute of Technology
Karlskrona, Sweden

Manuel Wimmer (ID)
Johannes Kepler University Linz
Linz, Austria

Johannes Bergsmann
Software Quality Lab GmbH
Linz, Austria

ISSN 1865-1348 ISSN 1865-1356 (electronic)
Lecture Notes in Business Information Processing
ISBN 978-3-030-65853-3 ISBN 978-3-030-65854-0 (eBook)
https://doi.org/10.1007/978-3-030-65854-0

This Springer imprint is published by the registered company Springer Nature Switzerland AG
The registered company address is: Gewerbestrasse 11, 6330 Cham, Switzerland

Preface

Message from the General Chair

The Software Quality Days (SWQD) conference and tools fair was first organized in 2009 and has since grown to be the largest yearly conference on software quality in Europe with a strong and vibrant community. The program of the SWQD conference was designed to encompass a stimulating mixture of practice-oriented presentations, scientific presentations of new research topics, tutorials, and an exhibition area for tool vendors and other organizations in the area of software quality.

This professional symposium and conference offered a range of comprehensive and valuable opportunities for advanced professional training, new ideas, and networking with a series of keynote speeches, professional lectures, exhibits, and tutorials.

The SWQD conference welcomes anyone interested in software quality including: software process and quality managers, test managers, software testers, product managers, agile masters, project managers, software architects, software designers, requirements engineers, user interface designers, software developers, IT managers, release managers, development managers, application managers, and many more.

The guiding conference topic of the SWQD 2021 was "What's The Next Big Thing in Software Engineering and Quality?" as changed product, process, and service requirements, e.g., distributed engineering projects, mobile applications, involvement of heterogeneous disciplines and stakeholders, extended application areas, and new technologies include new challenges and might require new and adapted methods and tools to support quality activities early in the software life cycle.

January 2021   Johannes Bergsmann

Message from the Scientific Program Chairs

The 13th Software Quality Days (SWQD 2021) conference and tools fair brought together researchers and practitioners from business, industry, and academia working on quality assurance and quality management for software engineering and information technology. The SWQD conference is one of the largest software quality conferences in Europe.

Over the past years, we have received a growing number of scientific contributions to the SWQD symposium. Starting back in 2012, the SWQD symposium included a dedicated scientific program published in scientific proceedings. In this 10th edition, we received an overall number of 13 high-quality submissions from researchers across Europe which were each peer-reviewed by 4 or more reviewers. Out of these submissions, we selected 3 contributions as full papers, yielding an acceptance rate of 23%. Further, we accepted 5 short papers representing promising research directions to spark discussions between researchers and practitioners on promising work in progress. This year, we introduced two interactive sessions: One on Quality Assurance for Artificial Intelligence, to emphasis future directions in Software Quality supported by paper contributions, and another one on Academia Industry Collaborations, not supported by paper contributions. Furthermore, we have two scientific keynote speakers for the scientific program, who contributed two invited papers. Tony Gorschek from Blekinge Institute of Technology, Sweden, elaborates further on the role and relevance of empirical software engineering to foster academia-industry collaborations, and Henning Femmer from Qualicen GmbH, Germany, elaborates on the future role of a requirements engineer in light of the ever-growing automation in today's engineering processes.

Main topics from academia and industry focused on Systems and Software Quality Management Methods, Improvements of Software Development Methods and Processes, latest trends and emerging topics in Software Quality, and Testing and Software Quality Assurance.

This book is structured according to the sessions of the scientific program following the guiding conference topic "Future Perspectives on Software Engineering Quality":

- Automation in Software Engineering
- Quality Assurance for AI-Based Systems
- Machine Learning Applications
- Industry-Academia Collaboration
- Experimentation in Software Engineering

January 2021

Stefan Biffl
Dietmar Winkler
Daniel Mendez
Manuel Wimmer

Organization

SWQD 2021 was organized by the Software Quality Lab GmbH, Germany, the Vienna University of Technology, Institute of Information Systems Engineering, Austria, the Blekinge Institute of Technology, Sweden, and the Johannes Kepler University Linz, Austria.

Organizing Committee

General Chair

Johannes Bergsmann   Software Quality Lab GmbH, Austria

Scientific Program Co-chair

Stefan Biffl   TU Wien, Austria
Dietmar Winkler   TU Wien, Austria
Daniel Mendez   Blekinge Institute of Technology, Sweden, and fortiss
                                      GmbH, Germany
Manuel Wimmer   Johannes Kepler University Linz, Austria

Proceedings Chair

Dietmar Winkler   TU Wien, Austria

Organizing and Publicity Chair

Petra Bergsmann   Software Quality Lab GmbH, Austria

Program Committee

SWQD 2021 established an international committee of well-known experts in software quality and process improvement to peer review the scientific submissions.

Maria Teresa Baldassarre   University of Bari, Italy
Tomas Bures   Charles University, Czech Republic
Matthias Book   University of Iceland, Iceland
Ruth Breu   University of Innsbruck, Austria
Maya Daneva   University of Twente, The Netherlands
Deepak Dhungana   University of Applied Sciences, Austria
Frank Elberzhager   Fraunhofer IESE, Germany
Michael Felderer   University of Innsbruck, Austria
Henning Femmer   Qualicen GmbH, Germany
Gordon Fraser   University of Passau, Germany
Nauman Ghazi   Blekinge Institute of Technology, Sweden
Volker Gruhn   University of Duisburg-Essen, Germany

Contents

Industry-Academia Collaboration

Experimentation in Software Engineering

Automation in Software Engineering

Assisted Requirements Engineering - What Will Remain in the Hands of the Future Requirements Engineer? (Invited Keynote)

Henning Femmer[✉][iD]

Qualicen GmbH, München, Germany
henning.femmer@qualicen.de

Abstract. Requirements engineering (RE) is widely considered one of the most difficult and risky activities in software and systems engineering. Since RE requires communication, and despite other ideas and experiments, tasks around textual content remains at the center of the RE for most projects. With a daily evolving field of natural language processing (NLP), the question is: Which of these tasks will - independent from any technological and methodological advancements - stay in the hands of the requirements engineer and which tasks will be automated?

This paper will take a look into the crystal ball. Based on analogies from programming and autonomous driving, and based on an analysis of the abilities of NLP and abilities of other modern technologies, I present a vision of the life of a future requirements engineer.

Keywords: Requirements engineering · Automatic methods · Natural Language Processing

1 Introduction: The World is Changing, RE is Changing, So What Will Remain?

Never before in the history of mankind have we had such a rapid evolution of products in such short time. The invention of the automobile in the late 19th century set off a chain reaction of technological changes that have profoundly reshaped the world. The invention of electricity in the early 20th century was the final catalyst for the rapid evolution of our world. In the 20th century, we developed the world 's most advanced and efficient communication network. By the 1970s, we had the world 's first computer. In the 80's, we moved on to the internet and by the 1990 1990s, we moved onto mobile phones and smart phones. In 2000, we reached a point where we have a smartphone that has become the most important communications device in our lives. Now we are looking at an almost limitless amount of potential for technology that will transform our world for the better.

© Springer Nature Switzerland AG 2021
D. Winkler et al. (Eds.): SWQD 2021, LNBIP 404, pp. 3–14, 2021.
https://doi.org/10.1007/978-3-030-65854-0_1

So much so, that in the previous paragraph I only wrote the first sentence and generated the remaining part through the software system GPT-2 [21]. In the software world, new computational powers through evolution of hardware, data centers, powerful abstractions in computer languages and reusable software libraries enable to build systems which relieve humans from an increasing number of tasks. Similarly, in the systems engineering world, sensors enable systems to recognize the world and interact with the world more like us. For example, in the automotive industry we do now have cars which first assisted the driver and now little-by-little replace them. If this happens in a way that was previously considered to be not possible to automate, we speak of *Artificial Intelligence* [1]. All in all, we see that we are building more and more powerful systems, of which many are build to automate tasks previously executed by humans.

At the same time, another technological shift changed requirements engineering. Previously, bug fixing an existing system was a cumbersome and expensive endeavor. For many systems today, bug fixing is just a commit, which automatically redeploys the software to the users. This all of a sudden made fast feedback loops with users possible that would have been unthinkable before. If you can improve, getting it wrong is no longer a project failure. This change questioned the whole requirements engineering paradigm which ultimately is just a means, but not an end, on the way to the real system, i.e. source code.

Now, that most of the engineering world is in motion, we are at a pivotal moment to shape the future of RE. Will it become a forgotten technique, or will it redefine itself? Which are tasks that - with current technologies or technologies that are imaginable today - can be executed by computers? Where are domains where computers, much like driver assistance functions in cars, can simplify the tasks? And finally, where is the human to our current understanding irreplaceable and always will be?

If you're looking for evidence, sorry, wrong paper. This paper is a personal opinion and just spells out one vision of what is possible. It is intended to serve as a hypothesis, not as an argument. As such it updates previous outlooks into the future, such as the ones by Nuseibeh and Easterbrook [20], Finkelstein and Emmerich [9], or Cheng and Atlee [3]. Looking at recent visions, there are people discussing the outlook on various topics such as Crowd-based RE [16], Data-Driven RE [19]. Obviously also tool vendors think into these directions, for example by Jama Software [23].

2   Which Steps Do Automations Take? Some Analogies

As previously mentioned, never before in the history did we have this extraordinary evolution in technology. Therefore, the best analogies are close to our current time. In the following, I describe the evolution in two areas, namely Programming Software and Assisted Automotive Driving.

We will see that in both analogies, we start with very solution oriented ways to solve the problem. The evolution goes through the following steps (see Fig. 1):

---

[1] "Artificial intelligence is the science and engineering of making computers behave in ways that, until recently, we thought required human intelligence." [13].

First, a very solution-oriented way to achieve a task is found. The steps to achieve the actual goal must be found and executed by a human, usually with plenty of manual work. Next, a form of indirection is introduced that enables to separate the actual task from the physical work. This enables the third step, where now humans are supported through assistance functions that warn them about dangerous behavior, e.g. a car appearing in a blind spot. This leads to the fourth step, where simple tasks are executed by the automated system, such as emergency braking. Finally, we have a 6th step, where the human only focuses on the actual goal of the task, while the necessary means to get there are defined and executed by a computer system.

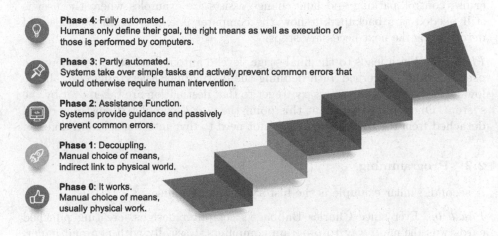

Phase 4: Fully automated.
Humans only define their goal, the right means as well as execution of those is performed by computers.

Phase 3: Partly automated.
Systems take over simple tasks and actively prevent common errors that would otherwise require human intervention.

Phase 2: Assistance Function.
Systems provide guidance and passively prevent common errors.

Phase 1: Decoupling.
Manual choice of means, indirect link to physical world.

Phase 0: It works.
Manual choice of means, usually physical work.

Fig. 1. Automation phases

2.1 Driver Assistance

Phase 0: The road that was taken by automotive drivers started with the drivers task to manually move the vehicle into the right direction: The first cars were equipped with tillers for steering [25]. As an explanation, one can find that at the time this was the way to steer carriages and most boats and this was therefore the most obvious solution. I want to add that this is also the most solution-oriented way to steer in the sense that it is closest to steering the raw engine power. In other words, the design of the system, not the goal of the driver, dominates the user interaction.

Phase 1: In the next evolution, car designers abstracted from directing the forces and looked closer at the needs of the driver. The new steering wheels, again taken from ship designs, enabled to more directly influence the direction of driving instead of the direction of raw forces, focusing a little further on the problem domain. It furthermore enabled a large set of follow-up evolutions.

Phase 2: Then came the time of assistance functions: The vehicle designers were now free from the raw forces and able to add functionality independent from the original mechanics of the system. Starting with adjustable steering wheels, the wheels were most prominently enhanced by power steering, which was ultimately perfected with drive-by-wire systems. Drive-by-wire is, technically, completely detached from the necessities of the solution domain. This abstraction then gives opportunities to support and manipulate the actions. Blind spot and distance warning systems are among the more recently introduced functions. Here, the user must still execute tasks within the realm of the traffic situation, but the computer makes sure that every action taken by the human is happening within a safe space.

Phase 3: Now we're seeing the system taking over in simple tasks. E.g. adaptive cruise control, parking and lane change assists are examples where the user is still needed as a backup, but now the computer is executing the actions and determining the next necessary steps.

Phase 4: Which leads to the final stage, level-6 autonomous driving, where the users are only concerned with defining the destination. Everything else, all the low-level steps that are necessary to get to that destination are taken over by the system. One could say, that at this point the user is completely abstracted and detached from the solution and does not need to dive into the solution domain.

2.2 Programming

A second, similar example is the history of programming.

Phase 0: Ever since Charles Babbage's computer designs, creating punched cards was the main way to program computers. Basically with pen and paper, programmers had very little technical support. As with driving, the design of punch cards was dominated by the physical reality of the solution (i.e. the punch card processing computer), not by the necessities of the programmer.

Phase 1: Along came digital file systems, programming with text editors and digital compilers. They abstracted from the raw powers of computers and thereby enabled programmers to reuse and exchange files more easily. Most fundamentally, however, programming systems within the computer itself, but detached from the physical reality now enabled computer-assisted programming.

Phase 2: The rise of IDEs (integrated development environment) is attributed to Borland with their TurboPascal editor in the 80ies, as well as Microsoft's Visual Basic in '91. Among other things, these new tools provided assistance in various areas: Syntax highlighting, rapid compiler feedback, resource organization, refactoring and more. Similar to blind spot warning systems, IDEs can sound an alarm when the programming is about to make a mistake.

Phase 3: In our current programming world, assistance systems have become ubiquitous during programming. It starts with static analysis tools indicating potential issues such as security threats [18] or maintainability issues [12]. But those systems do not remain passive anymore. Modern IDEs are equipped with recommender systems which basically aim at being one step ahead of the programmers, taking some mental load of their minds and making their day-to-day work less complex. In a way, these next level assistance functions are similar to lane change assistance functions in car, in that they take away simple tasks from the programmers, while still forcing them to come up with the individual steps to achieve their goal.

Phase 4: Now the final stage, again, can only be programmers expressing what they need and leaving the "pathfinding" to the system. As an outlook, we have just recently seen the ability of deep learning networks to transform natural language text into code [22]. Albeit much further from that goal than say current cars from Level-6-Autonomous Driving, this would represent the final level of abstraction.

3 Text Analytics Revisited: What is, Will, and Will Never Be Possible?

In the following, I want to shed a light on what automation can potentially do with text. For this, we could look at the abilities of various Natural Language Processing (NLP) APIs. However, to our end, let us focus on the problem domain that is addressed (which we call *text analytics*), instead of focusing on how a problem is addressed in the solution domain of NLP. The following sections will first look into challenges and limitations of text analytics with regards to requirements engineering. The section afterwards will discuss the potentials and look at the stakeholders and uses cases of text analytics as we see it today.

3.1 What Will Not Change Despite of Text Analytics?

In a previous study [5], we analyzed to which extent checking requirements guidelines could be automated. To this end, we went through a large guideline with more than 100 rules and decomposed it even further until we faced only atomic rules. We then independently classified what is, what could and what would never be possible to automate. Even though also the quantitative findings were interesting since it revealed a substantial potential for automation in checking guidelines, the qualitative findings are more applicable to our question. The analysis indicated the following reasons why rules were challenging to automate[2]:

Unclear or imprecise: If the task is subjective, and different humans cannot agree which solution is correct, then this will be challenging to automate. An example of this is the question whether a requirement is *well-written*.

---

[2] Please note that these are challenges in the sense that in individual cases you can still overcome the challenge but in the very most situations the solution will be inherently incomplete or imprecise.

Deep semantic understanding: If the task requires knowledge about the actual semantics of the text, full understanding of semantics of phrases, perfect coreference resolution across full texts, ability to deduce the logical meaning from the sentences grammar, etc. this is still far away and unclear whether it will be possible to reach at all. An example of this is the question whether a set of requirements is *consistent*.

Profound domain knowledge: If the task requires deep knowledge about which solutions are optimal inside a specific context, and this context is not available in any form of data, this might indicate a challenge as well. An example of this is the question whether a set of requirements is *implementable*.

Process status knowledge: If the task requires knowledge that is acquired in informal and undocumented ways, such as discussions during coffee, this would also make automatic analysis impossible. An example of this is the question whether the status of a requirement is *up-to-date*.

In addition to the challenges above, there is one item which makes it absolutely impossible to automate.

System scope knowledge: If the task touches anything about the actual goal of the system, this task remains impossible to automate. This is comparable to a level-6 automotive driving solution, which cannot tell the driver where they want to go. An example of this is the question whether a set of requirements is *correct and complete*.

Despite the list being created with a different question in mind (*Which requirements guideline rules can be automatically checked?*) I have been applying it in various text analytics project discussions in practice. Therefore, it might be useful also here in order to understand what will remain with the requirements engineer.

3.2   What Could Change with Text Analytics?

To discuss how RE could change, we also have to look at what's possible. For this, we have to discuss the generic stakeholders and their potential use cases of text analytics.

The four generic stakeholders for any form of text, as illustrated in Fig. 2, are writers, readers, users (anybody who uses the text as an input to a follow-up activity), and quality or supervisor people, who are not necessarily interested in reading the text itself but only want to make sure that the quality is adequate.

The use cases of text analytics for these roles are the following:

Writers: provide feedback while writing. The most obvious use case is concerned with assisting the author of a text. Here, a text analytics solution can provide fast, cheap and consistent (including unbiased) feedback, for example to support terminological work, unambiguity, and more (see e.g. [4]). Various common NLP tasks, such as morphological analysis [15] or others are required for this text analytics use case.

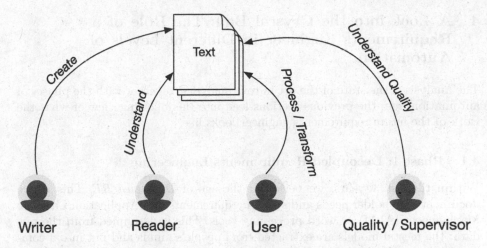

Fig. 2. Text analytics stakeholders

Writers: generate text. The use case which probably gets the most attention at the moment is the text generation use case. Here, GPT-3 [1] creates astonishing texts. However, it is still unclear how the incredible text generation skills can be steered into the intention of the writer, so that the automation does not just create any readable text, but instead the text that the writer intends.

Readers: find information. Readers want to first find, but ultimately extract a piece of information from a text. Finding usually refers to defined concepts, such as a specific product. The piece of information to extract can be either a fact such as a name, date or value, or it can be a relationship, e.g. which versions of the product were produced where.

Users: transform relevant information into new artifacts. Users of the text go one step further: Not only do they want to acquire a certain information, but they want to use that knowledge to generate the next artifact. For example, testers reads a requirements artifact, apply their testing methodology and thus create test cases (see [10,11]).

QA: Overview large pieces of text. Lastly, there are various roles who are not really interested in the contents of the actual artifacts. All they care about is that the artifacts fulfill a specific quality definition. This definition can be either a standard, such as ISO/IEEE/IEC-29148 [14], or it is something along the lines of *it must be usable* leading to a quality-in-use definition of quality [6].

4 A Look into the Crystal Ball: The Role of a Requirements Engineer in Different Levels of Automation

The analysis of the state of the art in text analytics, together with the phases of automation from the previous sections feed into the following view of what the work of the future requirements engineer looks like.

4.1 Phase 1: Decoupled Requirements Engineering

Within the last 30 years, we perfected the age of *Decoupled RE*. This is, we document stakeholder needs and system requirements into Application Lifecycle Management (ALM) or word processing tools. This is decoupled from the raw data: the mental models are extracted from people's minds and put into a computer system. As discussed previously, this now enables all kinds of processing of that information.

4.2 Phase 2: Assistance Functions in Requirements Engineering

We're now peeking into a new phase: Projects in *Assisted RE* run very similarly to today's projects. REs will "stay in the driver seat" by still being the main actor in nearly all tasks:

- REs will select stakeholders and interview them, select further input sources for possible requirements (e.g. app reviews).
- They must also facilitate requirements prioritization.
- REs will document the extracted needs together with attributes, traces and further meta-information.
- REs must review for correctness, completeness, consistency and other attributes.

However, in addition, the system will support REs, e.g.:

- The system will point out identified ambiguities, semantic duplication, and more problems, either in documented text [4] or during direct communication [8,24].
- Furthermore, the system will ensure that the documented requirements follow defined quality guidelines, either constructively through pattern or structure mechanisms, or analytically through rule-based engines.
- The system will automatically suggest specific meta attributes [26] or traceability links.
- Lasttly, the system will automatically scan certain sources, such as App Reviews and identify possible requirements [2].

4.3   Phase 3: Partly Automated Requirements Engineering

After this, the automation will go one step further. Projects in *Partly Automated RE* are willing to give responsibility to automation for simpler scenarios.

For example, the system will support REs in the following ways:

– The system will visualize the information accessed from interviews, and suggest textual requirements.
– In addition, the system will suggest test cases based on requirements. Based on human demonstrations, the system will then learn about relevant features and (possibly semi-automatically) link these to the test cases. This would create maintenance-free fully-automated requirements-based system testing.

However, REs will still:

– REs will guide interviews and identify incompleteness.
– REs will proof-read all texts generated by the automation.
– REs will detect difficult inconsistencies or items that are outside of project scope or budget.

4.4   Phase 4: Fully Automated Requirements Engineering

In *Fully Automated RE*, Requirements Engineers are reduced to their facilitation role.

In addition to everything from Phase 3, the RE system will support REs as follows:

– The system will interactively execute interviews with the stakeholders, record their responses, and visualize back to the stakeholders what it understood. If answers are unclear, it will request clarifications.
– The system will generate a model of how each of the stakeholders perceive the problem and what each of the stakeholders expects from the solution.[3] The model will most probably be based on transfer learning and not start at zero, but instead start with pretrained models for different applications, e.g. automotive, healthcare, insurance etc.
– The system will allow interactively requesting information of all kinds from this system. Since real world systems have allegedly crossed the mark of one million requirements, we will soon need to find new ways of structuring information. One possible answer is to not structure the information manually beforehand, but instead build a highly capable query language to extract and structure the information on the go, based on the current use case.
– Based on its knowledge model, the system will identify inconsistencies, and request the stakeholders to resolve them.

Ultimately, in the hands of the RE remains only:

---

[3] Please note that, due to the other abilities, this model no longer needs to be written in a human-readable language.

- REs will identify the goal of the project and guide the discussion through prototyping.
- REs will prioritize the suggested stakeholders and define their relevance for the project.
- REs will analyse and manage risks.
- REs will identify which parts of the system are possible to implement within the system scope.
- REs will identify potential reuse and its impact on the project scope.
- Through their knowledge of what's possible, REs will identify smart creative functional solutions on how to address a certain customer need (functional creativity) and steer the system by feeding it these creative ideas.[4]

Obviously, as of today, these are very bold statements and to which extent they will be possible to fully implement remains very unclear. In addition, similar to the autonomous driving case, we also have to consider the consequences of such a high level of automation and ask whether we want to go this way. In particular, this has also an ethical dimension. Who is liable if things go wrong?

5   Summary and Outlook

Most requirements engineers today are still heavily relying on gut feeling and manual work to execute their day to day work. This paper illustrates how in other applications, namely steering a car and programming, the computer gradually took over task by task, until the activity is reduced to its core.

Based on those examples, the paper continues to describe different ages of requirements engineering. Right now - at least in requirements engineering in industry - we're still in the age of *Decoupled RE*. In research and partly in practice, we're seeing the dawn of *Assisted RE*, with more and more support from computer systems. First ideas exist towards *Partly Automated RE*, where simpler tasks are executed by the computer with the RE only watching. Lastly, very few time has been spent on the vision of a *Fully Automated RE*, where a computer system (or model) becomes the source of knowledge that is able to digest various types of information and transform it just-in-time according to the needs of the consumer.

Not discussed in this work is - besides minor questions about how we are actually going to achieve this - the question of what should be done first. Of course, this is ultimately a cost-benefit-analysis. Here, two lines of thought are possible: First, we should automate what is laying in front of us. Automatic quality feedback mechanism are probably among those. But second, we should also focus on risk: Based on necessary empirical evidence about what are the most risky aspects of aforementioned analysis (e.g. from NAPIRE reports [7]), research will continue to focus on those most important aspects.

---

[4] Note that here the role of a RE is not passive consumption and documentation of information, but the very active role of a digital designer, c.f. [17] (in German).

Acknowledgments. I would like to thank Daniel Mendez and Jannik Fischbach for their feedback and opinion on the ideas as well as early drafts of this paper.

References

1. Brown, T.B., et al.: Language models are few-shot learners. arXiv preprint arXiv:2005.14165 (2020)
2. Carreño, L.V.G., Winbladh, K.: Analysis of user comments: an approach for software requirements evolution. In: 2013 35th International Conference on Software Engineering (ICSE), pp. 582–591. IEEE (2013)
3. Cheng, B.H., Atlee, J.M.: Research directions in requirements engineering. In: Future of Software Engineering (FOSE 2007), pp. 285–303. IEEE (2007)
4. Femmer, H., Méndez Fernández, D., Wagner, S., Eder, S.: Rapid quality assurance with requirements smells. J. Syst. Softw. (2017). https://doi.org/10.1016/j.jss.2016.02.047
5. Femmer, H., Unterkalmsteiner, M., Gorschek, T.: Which requirements artifact quality defects are automatically detectable? a case study. In: 2017 IEEE 25th International Requirements Engineering Conference Workshops (REW), pp. 400–406. IEEE (2017)
6. Femmer, H., Vogelsang, A.: Requirements quality is quality in use. IEEE Softw. **36**(3), 83–91 (2018)
7. Fernández, D.M.: Supporting requirements-engineering research that industry needs: the napire initiative. IEEE Softw. **1**, 112–116 (2018)
8. Ferrari, A., Spoletini, P., Gnesi, S.: Ambiguity and tacit knowledge in requirements elicitation interviews. Requirements Eng. **21**(3), 333–355 (2016). https://doi.org/10.1007/s00766-016-0249-3
9. Finkelstein, A., Emmerich, W.: The future of requirements management tools. In: Oesterreichische Computer Gesellschaft (Austrian Computer Society) (2000)
10. Fischbach, J., Vogelsang, A., Spies, D., Wehrle, A., Junker, M., Freudenstein, D.: Specmate: automated creation of test cases from acceptance criteria. In: 2020 IEEE 13th International Conference on Software Testing, Validation and Verification (ICST), pp. 321–331. IEEE (2020)
11. Freudenstein, D., Junker, M., Radduenz, J., Eder, S., Hauptmann, B.: Automated test-design from requirements-the specmate tool. In: 2018 IEEE/ACM 5th International Workshop on Requirements Engineering and Testing (RET), pp. 5–8. IEEE (2018)
12. Heinemann, L., Hummel, B., Steidl, D.: Teamscale: Ssoftware quality control in real-time. In: Companion Proceedings of the 36th International Conference on Software Engineering, pp. 592–595 (2014)
13. High, P.: Carnegie Mellon Dean Of Computer Science On The Future Of AI (2017). https://www.forbes.com/sites/peterhigh/2017/10/30/carnegie-mellon-dean-of-computer-science-on-the-future-of-ai/#3747e3b62197
14. ISO, IEC, IEEE: ISO/IEC/IEEE 29148:2018-Systems and software engineering - Life cycle processes - Requirements engineering. Technical report, ISO IEEE IEC (2018)
15. Jurafsky, D., Martin, J.H.: Speech and Language Processing. 2nd edn. Pearson Education, London (2014)

16. Khan, J.A., Liu, L., Wen, L., Ali, R.: Crowd intelligence in requirements engineering: current status and future directions. In: Knauss, E., Goedicke, M. (eds.) REFSQ 2019. LNCS, vol. 11412, pp. 245–261. Springer, Cham (2019). https://doi.org/10.1007/978-3-030-15538-4_18
17. Lauenroth, K., Lehn, K., Trapp, M., Schubert, U.: Digital design-der nächste schritt für das requirements engineering im kontext der digitalen transformation (in German) (2017)
18. Livshits, V.B., Lam, M.S.: Finding security vulnerabilities in java applications with static analysis. USENIX Secur. Symp. **14**, 18–18 (2005)
19. Maalej, W., Nayebi, M., Johann, T., Ruhe, G.: Toward data-driven requirements engineering. IEEE Softw. **33**(1), 48–54 (2015)
20. Nuseibeh, B., Easterbrook, S.: Requirements engineering: a roadmap. In: Proceedings of the Conference on the Future of Software Engineering, pp. 35–46 (2000)
21. Radford, A., Wu, J., Child, R., Luan, D., Amodei, D., Sutskever, I.: Language models are unsupervised multitask learners. OpenAI Blog **1**(8), 9 (2019)
22. sharifshameem: Twitter. (2020). https://twitter.com/sharifshameem/status/1284421499915403264?s=20/. Accessed 27 Aug 2020
23. Software, J.: What is the future of requirements management? (2020). https://www.jamasoftware.com/blog/what-is-the-future-of-requirements-management/ (2020). Accessed 27 Aug 2020
24. Spoletini, P., Brock, C., Shahwar, R., Ferrari, A.: Empowering requirements elicitation interviews with vocal and biofeedback analysis. In: 2016 IEEE 24th International Requirements Engineering Conference (RE), pp. 371–376 (2016)
25. Wikipedia: Steering Wheel (2020). https://en.wikipedia.org/wiki/Steering_wheel/. Accessed 27 Aug 2020
26. Winkler, J., Vogelsang, A.: Automatic classification of requirements based on convolutional neural networks. In: 2016 IEEE 24th International Requirements Engineering Conference Workshops (REW), pp. 39–45 (2016)

Testing Autogenerated OPC UA NodeSet Models for Product Variants in Industry

Claus Klammer[1][✉], Thomas Wetzlmaier[1], Michael Pfeiffer[1], Thomas Steiner[2], and Matthias Konnerth[2]

[1] Software Competence Center Hagenberg GmbH, Hagenberg, Austria
{claus.klammer,thomas.wetzlmaier,michael.pfeiffer}@scch.at
[2] ENGEL Austria GmbH, Schwertberg, Austria
{thomas.steiner,matthias.konnerth}@engel.at

Abstract. Product line management activities have to ensure that offered product options are valid and compatible. With the arise of the Internet of Things (IoT) movement not only the own product compatibility has to be managed by the vendors anymore, but also the compliance and openness to standardized interfaces has to be supported as well. The Machine to Machine (M2M) communication protocol standard Open Platform Communications Unified Architecture (OPC UA) has received great attention in the field of mechanical engineering recently. In this industrial experience report we describe our approach how to support the testing of automatically generated models for OPC UA, by applying test case generation at the integration level. We show the feasibility of our approach and report about found issues, discuss some general findings and provide an outlook for future work.

Keywords: Middleware · Integration testing · Test case generation · OPC UA

1 Introduction

With the internet, as global standardized available communication channel, not only human can now collaborate with each other easily regardless their location, but also production processes and dependent services can exchange data easily. Building upon this idea, the Internet of Things (IoT) movement draws the vision of interconnected things, where so-called smart sensors are connected to the internet [1]. However, in the traditional manufacturing domain there exist older communication technologies and protocols to connect sensors and actors to a program logic control (PLC) unit of a machine or device. Extension or integration of additional hardware components, even from other vendors, is difficult since they may use different interfaces starting from the physical layer up to the protocol layer. With the increasing pressure towards better support of Machine to Machine (M2M) communication, the existing Open Platform Communications (OPC) standard has been evolved to Open Platform Communications Unified

© Springer Nature Switzerland AG 2021
D. Winkler et al. (Eds.): SWQD 2021, LNBIP 404, pp. 15–29, 2021.
https://doi.org/10.1007/978-3-030-65854-0_2

Architecture (OPC UA)[1]. OPC UA is the enabling technology for flexible, adaptive, and transparent production [2,3]. It provides the technological foundation, based on standard internet technologies, to build up standardized information models for a specific domain to ensure interoperability between different vendors.

However, in order to support these standardized information models every manufacturer has to provide an adapter for the existing middleware or control program to join these worlds. The OPC UA standard defines different approaches to provide the required model instance. One is to provide a so-called NodeSet file, which is an xml file whose structure is specified by an xml schema file. For instance, such information model descriptions provide the program variables to be published via OPC UA middleware. Vendors of OPC UA servers provide modeling tools that support the creation of such adapters. However, such a manual approach is only feasible in the context of small, more or less static control programs. In recent years control programs grew in size and complexity and often the numbers of variations and options are even reflected in modularized and customized control programs. To manage these available options and link them to appropriate software components, many companies apply tools that automate such tasks and support the product line management. The provided models for the OPC UA middleware have to match the underlying control program. Therefore, there is a need to automatically generate most models for different variants and order-specific control programs. All information required for the generation of corresponding NodeSets has to be available within the control program. That assuming, the next question is how to ensure that the generation process creates correct NodeSets for any thinkable control program.

The objective of this paper is to describe our approach how to support the testing of automatically generated models for OPC UA, by applying test case generation at the integration level. Besides the goal of communicating the implementation of the approach and demonstrating its basic feasibility, we will answer the main research question:

Which Issues Will Our Generative Testing Approach Find in Its Productive Application? Therefore we analyze the executed test runs and discuss found issues. The answer to this question is important to assess the potential of the approach and to derive tasks for its further development.

The remainder of this paper is structured as follows. Section 2 provides the industrial context and some references to related literature motivating our testing approach. Afterwards the approach and its implementation are presented in Sect. 3. The results and the discussion of the research question and additional findings are provided in Sect. 4 and the paper ends with the conclusion and outlook in Sect. 5.

2   Industrial Context and Related Work

ENGEL Austria GmbH (ENGEL) is a world-leading manufacturer of injection molding machines. With about 6900 employees worldwide, the company pro-

---

[1] https://reference.opcfoundation.org/.

duces ma-chines and automation solutions for the plastics processing industry. Its products are known for high quality and support of custom features. The product range covers small, individually operating machines up to large, complex production lines including robots and support for additional equipment from other manufacturers. The software from control level to human machine interface (HMI) level is component oriented, to support all these different machine features. New major versions of the software stack are released twice a year. For every order, the selected features and options define which software components are required. In addition, customer specific software components are implemented and provided when needed. This high flexibility and customization ability are supported by semi-automatic processes, which ensure the composition of the right software component versions and its dependencies. ENGEL has developed over the last years a static code analysis (SCA) platform for the used control program language Kemro IEC 61131-3 [4]. The core of the platform is the parser that transforms programs into a corresponding abstract syntax tree (AST) and allows the implementation of so-called meta programs with the Java programming language. Meta programs are tools, which read sentences of software languages, like IEC 61131-3 defined languages, and produce any kind of output [5]. All static analyses and calculations can be implemented in the high-level language Java and are performed on the AST representation provided by the SCA platform. This syntax tree also contains the information about the variables to be exposed to the middleware. Obviously, this established platform is used to generate the required NodeSet files for the new OPC UA based solution. A patent application was submitted for this meta program by ENGEL [6] recently. The development of this generator approach has been supported by manually prepared control programs and its appropriate resulting NodeSet files. Every of these control programs focuses on one specific feature of the exported NodeSet, e.g. to support variables of the type array. This way, step by step development and enhancement of the generator was supported by a safety-net of manually created and maintained control programs. Although this approach was fine for the start of the generator development, it soon became clear that changes in the generator causes high maintenance effort of the effected test control programs. Furthermore, the complexity of the data structures to be exported and all possibilities of the control program language to define and reference such structures cannot be covered by handmade test programs. Therefore, the question was how we could provide a denser safety net supporting the ongoing development with automation.

Grammar based test input generation is a research field with a 50 year long history [7]. It is a preferred approach for testing meta programs. Unfortunately, random generation of test input for big languages is not effective and often results in poor coverage of the tested meta program [8]. Hentz et al. [9] propose an approach that tackles this problem. By extracting information of the used input patterns of the tested meta program they tried to reduce the cost of grammar based testing. The test input data generation is guided by this pattern information with the aim to generate a minimal amount of inputs that will cover the meta program. In contrast to their pattern coverage approach, our test case generation approach should follow a more imperative generation approach by implementing a custom-made program that generates test data for the actual test focus. There exist few works, which cover the testing of industrial automation software. Ramler et al. present a test automation approach in the field of PLC software, share learned lessons and provide some recommendations [10]. Symbolic execution is applied by Suresh et al. [11] to create test cases for small PLC programs. However, they do not transfer this approach for testing meta programs targeting PLC programs. Pauker et al. report about a systematic approach to OPC UA information model design [12]. Model-driven architecture (MDA) as software development process is applied to create OPC UA information models. Though, the resulting workflow does not take into account the reverse, the creation and testing of the information model out of existing program code. González et al. provide a literature survey on the industrial application of OPC [13] and encourages the utilization of OPC UA to handle systems integration.

The Software Competence Center Hagenberg GmbH (SCCH) is a longtime partner of ENGEL for application-oriented research in the field of software quality and test automation, and has already gained experience and important insights into the application of test case generation at system level [14]. Therefore, we decided to work together on a solution to ensure the functionality of the generative approach for a broader range of programs.

3   Approach and Implementation

The main underlying idea of our solution is to automatically create test control pro-grams, perform the automatic node set generation and to check whether the resulting node sets files contain the expected data (Fig. 1). This cycle can then be repeated for a certain amount of time and failing projects are archived for later analyses.

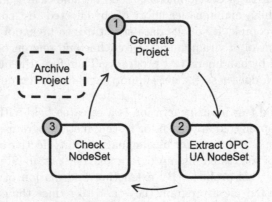

Fig. 1. Test cycle solution concept: generate PLC program project (1), extract OPC UA Nodeset (2), perform checks (3) and archive project in case of an test failure

Derived from the main idea our solution approach essentially consists of three building blocks, whose implementations are described later on. The test project generator (TPG) represents the core of our approach, since its purpose is to create valid control programs. The input data for the conformance test of the generated node sets, is provided by the test metadata exporter (TME) analyzing the generated control programs. The third building block is the test execution (TE), which uses the generated metadata to check the content of the exported node set files. Figure 2 provides an over-view of the integration of this building blocks into the existing NodeSet generation process.

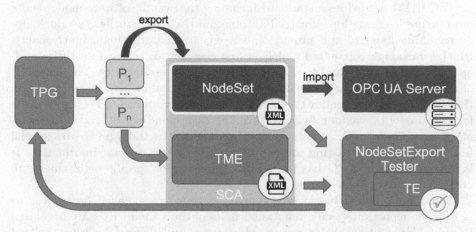

Fig. 2. Illustration of integrated main test building blocks: the color blue represents the added system parts for our test approach (Color figure online)

TPG with its generated control programs replaces real world, customized, production ready control programs. The static code analysis platform is utilized not only to generate the node sets, but also to extract the required control program metadata as xml file. The *NodeSetExportTester* implements and controls the test execution cycle by using the TPG, TME and TE. It uses the generated node sets, which are imported by the OPC UA server normally, and exported test metadata to perform conformance tests and to report the corresponding test results. The implementation of the solution has started with the implementation of the TPG in summer 2019. The first version of TPG was used by the development team to manually check for unknown use cases that were automatically generated by the tool but currently not supported by NodeSet generation. In parallel, the implementation of the metatdata exporter and corresponding test oracles started. It provides the basis for automatic testing of randomly created control programs by TPG. With the completion of its implementation an automatic test build job was configured that repeated the test cycle depicted in Fig. 1 for an hour every night and reported test failures. The node set generator is still in development and at the beginning of 2020 an extended version with additional tests has been set into production, which covers recently changed features of the node set generator.

3.1   Test Project Generator (TPG)

The purpose of the TPG is to generate valid, compilable Kemro IEC control programs that contain data that is intended to be exported by the node set exporter. In addition, every generated control program should be different. But configuration options should ensure that the generated control programs cover the features of the node set exporter since this is the software under test (SUT).

IEC 61131-3 provides a standard including the overall software model and a structuring language for industrial automation [15]. Nevertheless, vendors supporting this standard still provide enhancements and additional functionality, which for example is required to deliver first class editing support for their development environments and to increase development productivity. The downside of this situation is, that the vendor specific compiler often requires information that is created by its vendor specific development environment. This is also true for the used PLC vendor by ENGEL. The corresponding integrated development environment (IDE) assumes a certain folder structure and creates special files and sections in existing source files containing IDE specific information. It is obvious that our TPG has to consider these vendor specific requirements to create valid, compilable programs.

The main building blocks of a control program are so-called *function units* (FU) that represent specific functional units of the system. FUs are organized in subfolders and can reference variables from, and depend on types defined in, other function units. The random generation approach has to support the creation of several FUs and create types and use them by declared variables. As mentioned earlier data structures are marked within the source code, which is intended to be accessed via the middleware. This is achieved by adding a special attribute *VARIABLE_GROUP* with value *ComponentModel* to the variable. All variables marked with this attribute value are intended to be exported to the middleware. Besides, of the random assignment of this attribute for variables, the generator has to support this assignment also for structured datatypes like arrays and structs and complex custom data structures that mix and nest these basic data types.

The TPG has been implemented as a command line tool with the Java programming language, since also the developed Kemro IEC language parser has been developed in Java and the development team has years of development experience with the language. The generation process is divided into two steps (Fig. 3). Phase one, the generation phase, takes an optional xml file to configure the generation process and creates a model of a project regarding this configuration in memory. In phase two, the export phase, this internal representation is exported as folders and files to create the valid representation that is assumed by the used Kemro IEC programming language compiler and editor. At the end of this phase the project compiler is executed to ensure that the generated project is valid and that all files necessary for the subsequent node set export exist.

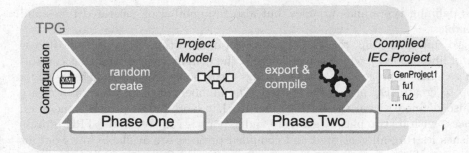

Fig. 3. TPG generation process overview

Phase One: In the generation phase a model has to be build up, which not only contains IEC source code, but that also allows the creation of the required project structure sup-ported by the targeted PLC vendor. TPG therefore defines its own model objects and reuses parts of the AST model provided by the language parser of the SCA platform previously mentioned. The random generation of the model is controlled via a set-tings file in xml notation. Configuration of the generation phase can be divided into following groups:

– *General properties:* The seed value of the used random number generator can be set. In addition, a name prefix for the generated projects can be set.
– *Generation constraints:* These properties define settings and boundaries considered during the generation of the test projects, like the minimum and maximum number of FUs to create, which data types should be considered, and valid value ranges for default data types and nesting depth for custom types.
– *Generation probabilities:* Probability-defining properties are used to control the generation of various aspects. For example, the probability to apply the export at-tribute can be set.

Phase Two: To create only valid, compilable projects, we had to investigate which source files and meta information is required by the compiler first. The IDE supports the feature to import plain IEC files into a project and adds the additional vendor specific meta information for these files automatically. We utilized this feature to avoid the need to generate IDE specific metadata ourselves. Fortunately, many of the required files that form a valid project are more or less static. Hence, we used template files as base for the generation of most of the required files. As template engine *velocity*[2] was used. To get a quick overview about the actual content of the generated project, a summary report with statistical data is generated at the end of the generation process. It provides basic counters about the generated project, like the number of FUs, number of

---

[2] https://velocity.apache.org/.

files defining types and variables, but also the number of generated types and variables.

To sum things up, the TPG uses an optional settings file specified as command line property, which is merged with the default settings and that controls the generation process. Resulting settings are exported for later reference and a loop to create IEC projects is started. The number range of projects to create is also defined within the settings file. In that loop TPG's project generation process with its two phases, generate and export, is run. When the TPG process finishes its run, all generated and compiled projects are available in its output directory. These projects are then the input for the TME to extract the information required for checking the generated OPC UA NodeSets.

3.2   Test Metadata Exporter (TME)

The SUT is the NodeSet exporter, which has been implemented as an extension of the utilized SCA platform. The SCA platform provides visitor hooks that allow the traversal of the AST of the parsed PLC program. Such implemented extensions (meta programs) are called rules, referring to the main purpose of the platform as static code analysis tool. Which rules are executed during a run of the SCA-Tool is configured by a configuration file in xml notation, in which the rules to be executed are listed by their identifier. If the NodeSet exporter rule, named *ExportOPCUANodeset*, is configured to be executed, the corresponding OPC UA NodeSet models are generated and exported in a folder called opcua next to the PLC program. To check the conformance of the exported NodeSet models to the PLC program, we have introduced the TME that is also implemented as SCA platform rule named *ExportOPCUAMetadata*. This rule is intended to provide all information that is required to check the conformance of the exported NodeSet model. The data is provided as one xml file per project, named *metadata.xml*, and saved within the project folder.

Currently the data structure is simple (Fig. 4) but sufficient to implement basic conformance tests. The root node of the file is named *metadata*. Its child nodes *fuData* groups the data of the exported variables by the projects FUs. The value of attribute *name* identifies the corresponding FU. All properties of every exported variable are listed under the node *varData*.

The TME rule implementation uses the given AST root node of a project to start with the data collection. Therefore, an instance of the implemented component *MetadataCollector* is created for the project internally, that is able to collect the metadata for every FU. It iterates over the variables and gathers metadata about variables that are marked to be intended to be exported to the middleware. The resulting xml file *metadata.xml* can then be used, to check the conformance of the exported OPC UA NodeSets.

```
<metadata>
  <fuData name="fu1">
    <varData>
      <name>sv_uVar14</name>
      <type>UDINT</type>
      <unit>Rotation</unit>
      <primitive>true</primitive>
      <reference>false</reference>
      <enum>false</enum>
    </varData>
    ...
  </fuData>
</metadata>
```

Fig. 4. Example excerpt of metadata.xml file

3.3   Test Execution (TE)

To check the conformance of the automatically generated NodeSets of a given PLC project, we implemented the tool *NodesetExportTester*. The tool starts the test cycle and runs the conformance checks.

An instance of an *OPCUAModelChecker* implements the comparison of the generated NodeSet xml files with the information provided by the given metadata file of one project. Currently, it supports two different test oracles. The first check allVariablesExported tests whether all variables are exported and available in the exported NodeSets and the second check allUnitsExported performs the same availability check for units. The overall check of the complete project fails if any check for any FU fails. The implementation provides an integration test that combines and utilizes TPG, SCA and the *OPCUAModelChecker* to create and execute automatic tests for the NodeSet exporter feature. *JUnit5*[3] supports the generation of tests during runtime by implementation of so-called *DynamicTests*. We use this feature to implement a test factory that creates and executes dynamic tests during its runtime for a specified time. Internally we use Java's pseudo random number generator to create the seed numbers to be used by the TPG to create different PLC projects for every test.

During test runtime, the test execution is performed according our solution approach depicted in Fig. 3 with following steps. At the start of every test cycle, the seed of the used configuration for the TPG is set to a unique value. Before starting with the project generation, all content of the defined output directory is removed, to ensure a clean project workspace. In the next step the TPG is called to create and prepare one random PLC project to the configured output directory. If an unexpected error occurs in this step, the test generation process is stopped and the test run is canceled. Otherwise the SCA platform is started and applied to the generated project afterwards with *ExportOPCUANodeset* and *ExportOPCUAMetadata* as the configured rules. The resulting output of this run

---
[3] https://junit.org/junit5/.

is used as the input for the final step. An instance of the *OPCUAModelChecker* is created and applied for this data. If the conformance test fails, the generated PLC project including the exported NodeSets and metadata are archived as zip compressed file for later analyses, before starting again with a new test creation cycle.

4   Results and Discussion

We provide general data about the executed test runs and present and discuss the found issues to answer our research question. Besides this discussion, we will share some general findings as result of the implementation and application of our automated test generation approach.

4.1   Test Execution Data

The analyzed time span of the provided data (Table 1) comprises eight months and starts with the first setup of the long running nightly test case generation build job. The data also contains some manually triggered builds, but the vast majority of the executed test runs were timed. Because of major refactorings of the NodeSet exporter, the execution of the test case generation was temporarily deactivated for two and a half months. This results in the total number of 194 executed test runs that are included in the analyzed data. Each test run was configured to create test cases for about one hour. 185 test runs ended successfully, i.e. have not been aborted or ended because of a build exception. Seven of these executions showed unstable behavior by at least one failing generated test case.

Table 1. Statistical data of build server test execution

Property	Value
Time span of collected data	8 month (August 2019–April 2020)
Configured test case generation duration (per test run)	3 600 s
Total number of executed test runs	194
Number of successful test run executions	185
Number of Passed/Unstable test runs	178/7
Number of Failed/Aborted test runs	8/1
Total number of generated test cases	36 640
Median number of generated test cases per successful test runs	204
Median execution time per test case	17.8 s
Number of real errors	2

Eight out of nine unsuccessful test runs were caused by compile errors of the test project, because of changed interfaces, and general network issues between the jenkins host and the executing test agent machine. Only one of the executed test runs was aborted manually. During these entire 185 successful test runs 36 640 test cases have been generated. The median of generated test cases per test run is 204. Generated violin plot in Fig. 5a depicts the deviation of the numbers of generated test cases for all test runs in the productive test infrastructure. About 17.8 s is the median execution time of all generated test cases. Its distribution is shown in Fig. 5b by the provided violin plot, with few, yet not examined outliers.

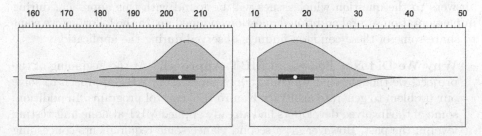

Fig. 5. a) distribution of generated test cases per test run and b) distribution of test case execution time in seconds

In the following we will discuss the main research question of this work: **Which issues will our generative testing approach find in its productive application?** Our approach is intended to provide a safety net for changes to the NodeSet exporter. Five of the seven failing test runs occurred at the beginning of the implementation of support for exposing variable's physical units. These changes introduced some general changes to the structure and content of the generated NodeSets. That is, our test case generation approach did not check the correct features of the exported NodeSet anymore and therefore this failed test runs do not indicate real issues. In contrast to this, the two remaining instable test runs revealed real issues, that the developers of the NodeSet exporter have not been aware at the time of its discovery. An exported variable would not have been available via the OPC UA server at runtime if one of these problems had not been detected. The first bug was detected on day two of the activation of the nightly test case generation build job. The current implementation of the NodeSet exporter did not consider annotations at the array index level as valid export annotations. About three weeks later the nightly test execution failed again. This time ongoing changes of the NodeSet exporter caused an issue with the resolution of array content types. To fix this issue the implementation of the NodeSet exporter had to be extended to also consider type references of multi dimensional arrays. The two problems found are special cases that have not been detected so far due to the complexity of the causing IEC code data structures. As above results show, our approach is able to find hidden problems and complement the set of manually created test cases. But we also have to admit that we only considered a relatively short period of application and that these are only preliminary results. In addition, we have added the manual written regression test series with tests that mimic this problem to avoid this kind of errors in the future. In this way, we are no longer dependent on the randomness of our approach to detect this concrete issues.

4.2   General Findings

We successfully applied our test case generation approach for building a safety net for the automatic generation of OPC UA NodeSets. Besides providing first answers to the question which issues will be found with this approach, during implementation several additional questions popped up. In the following we want to share some of these common findings observed during the application:

– **Why We Did Not Follow an MBT Approach?** At the beginning of the project, we thought that we could adopt an existing MBT approach to solve our problem to generate arbitrary Kemro IEC control programs. In addition, some of the involved developers had already applied MBT at none unit testing level in the past. However, at a second glance some requirements concerning the necessary configurability showed that the use and adaption of an existing tool would most probably require more effort with less implementation flexibility. Furthermore, if we look at the resulting approach, it is obvious that we do not dynamically test the features of our SUT (as intended by MBT), instead our solution is based on the data generator TPG and test oracle data collector TME and follows much more a data driven test approach.
– **How to Tackle the Problem of Reproducibility?** One of the most annoying problems in the context of test case generation is how the developer that should fix the problem can easily reproduce a revealed failure. Therefore, the test report provide all the necessary information. Our approach realizes this by archiving the generated test projects for failing tests. In addition, the base configuration with the used seed for the random number generator is saved in the case to regenerate the same IEC control program. Nevertheless, we also have to utilize tools of the IEC development environment during generation. We need these tools as external dependencies and newer versions might break the functionality of the implemented TPG because we depend on the vendor specific code parts and project structure.
– **How to Ensure and Assess Further Development of the Test Generation Approach?** In the last few years, the development process at ENGEL has transformed from a more or less waterfall approach to an agile, development sprint based process. For single developers and teams this means more freedom, but in turn also more responsibilities. Testing and its automation are tasks that are increasingly performed by the development team itself. Our integration testing approach has been implemented in parallel to the development of the OPC UA NodeSet exporter by different developers. The implemented and involved test infrastructure is quite complex. However, further development to support additional functionality of the NodeSet exporter

should be done by the core team in the future. Only the developers of additional features know whether it is worth to utilize such a test generation approach for specific features and which additional checks have to be implemented as the test oracle. Hence, we are convinced that the development team itself has to maintain the approach and drive its future development.

- **What is the Right Abstraction Level for Testing the Exported OPC UA NodeSet?** For this project, we tried to follow the most abstract path. The question about how concrete or abstract checks should be is one of the most challenging and controversially discussed questions. Nevertheless, the context of this project favors checks that are more abstract. The existence of handcrafted example projects, and its expected OPC UA NodeSet files, already assures the concrete representation of the expected NodeSet exporter output for these examples. This is achieved by structural comparison of the generated xml files. We argue that a generative test approach should only extend existing tests. If you try to generate test cases that are more concrete or test oracles automatically, you will have to provide a second implementation of the required features at the end, which might not be the intention of testing and what would cause much maintenance efforts in the future.

5   Conclusion and Outlook

In this paper we share our experiences in supporting the development of an automatic exporter of OPC UA NodeSets for arbitrary Kemro IEC control programs with automated testing. We presented the main idea to generate random PLC programs guided by a configuration and checking the conformance of the generated NodeSets afterwards automatically. The implementation of the main building blocks TPG, TME and TE is explained in detail and highlights the required automation effort. The results are discussed and show that the approach was able to uncover some regressions during the ongoing development of the NodeSet exporter. The problems found represent complex special cases that were previously not covered by manually implemented regression tests. Hence, we suggest the introduction of such a generative test approach for highly customizable software systems. Particularly its application will be beneficial for software in domains, where the quality of the product has to be ensured more thoroughly because the deployment of bug fixes is more difficult and expensive. Currently we are not aware of any publication that uses test case generation to test the conformance of automatically generated OPC UA information models. However, the implementation of this test generation approach also raised some additional questions, which should be addressed in future work:

- **How Could We Provide Any Quantitative Coverage Information About a Nightly Test Run?** Currently, only statistical information about the generated project and its content is reported. But we should investigate how and which coverage could be measured to get a clue about which portion of all possible IEC language features for a specific test generation configuration is covered. One possibility is to follow the pattern coverage approach by Hentz et al. [9].

- **Should the Test Generation Approach Also Consider Changing the Generation Configuration?** Our current test approach uses a fix configuration for the TPG. It determines the basic conditions of the generation and only the seed of used random generator is altered. The basic configuration is intended to produce the most realistic PLC programs. Nevertheless, it might be beneficial to alter this configuration with the hope to produce more unusual corner cases that might uncover unknown NodeSet exporter issues. Therefore, we should investigate how this alternation of the configuration can be realized and how it influences the bug-revealing capabilities of our approach.
- **Could Our Approach Be Extended to Ensure Compatibility Requirements of Generated NodeSet Models?** The NodeSet exporter will evolve in the future. New features will be added and existing ones changed, which will most likely also change the structure and content of the exported NodeSet files. Even new versions of or other standardized information models have to be supported in the future. Therefore, it is necessary to consider the compatibility requirements of these models and investigate how our test generation approach could provide support to ensure them.
- **How to Improve Maintainability of Our Approach?** Major refactorings of the code base of the NodeSet exporter broke our approach in the past. The existing implementation does not provide any other way than changing the source code to apply to the introduced changes and adapt to its changed behavior. An advanced version of our approach should be faster and easier to maintain, without the need to know the details of the underlying implementation. Hence, we have to explore and compare different possibilities to realize a much more flexible and adaptable solution first.

Acknowledgments. The research reported in this paper has been funded by the Federal Ministry for Climate Action, Environment, Energy, Mobility, Innovation and Technology (BMK), the Federal Ministry for Digital and Economic Affairs (BMDW), and the Province of Upper Austria in the frame of the COMET - Competence Centers for Excellent Technologies Programme managed by Austrian Research Promotion Agency FFG.

References

1. Al-Fuqaha, A., Guizani, M., Mohammadi, M., Aledhari, M., Ayyash, M.: Internet of Things: a survey on enabling technologies, protocols, and applications. IEEE Commun. Surv. Tutor. **17**(4), 2347–2376 (2015). https://ieeexplore.ieee.org/document/7123563/
2. Mahnke, W., Leitner, S.H., Damm, M.: OPC Unified Architecture. Springer, Berlin Heidelberg (2009). http://link.springer.com/10.1007/978-3-540-68899-0

3. Schleipen, M., Gilani, S.S., Bischoff, T., Pfrommer, J.: OPC UA & Industrie 4.0 - enabling technology with high diversity and variability. Procedia CIRP **57**, 315–320 (2016) http://www.sciencedirect.com/science/article/pii/S2212827116312094

4. Angerer, F., Prahofer, H., Ramler, R., Grillenberger, F.: Points-to analysis of IEC 61131–3 programs: implementation and application. In: 2013 IEEE 18th Conference on Emerging Technologies & Factory Automation (ETFA), pp. 1–8. IEEE, Cagliari, Italy (2013). http://ieeexplore.ieee.org/document/6648062/

5. Czarnecki, K., Eisenecker, U.: Generative Programming: Methods, Tools, and Applications. Addison Wesley, Boston (2000)

6. Engel Austria GmbH: a computer-implemented method to generate an OPC UA information model. EP19179350.4, submitted 11.06.2019

7. Hanford, K.V.: Automatic generation of test cases. IBM Syst. J. **9**(4), 242–257 (1970) http://ieeexplore.ieee.org/document/5388302/

8. Candea, G., Godefroid, P.: Automated software test generation: some challenges, solutions, and recent advances. In: Steffen, B., Woeginger, G. (eds.) Computing and Software Science. LNCS, vol. 10000, pp. 505–531. Springer, Cham (2019). https://doi.org/10.1007/978-3-319-91908-9_24

9. Hentz, C., Vinju, J.J., Moreira, A.M.: Reducing the cost of grammar-based testing using pattern coverage. In: El-Fakih, K., Barlas, G., Yevtushenko, N. (eds.) ICTSS 2015. LNCS, vol. 9447, pp. 71–85. Springer, Cham (2015). https://doi.org/10.1007/978-3-319-25945-1_5

10. Ramler, R., Putschögl, W., Winkler, D.: Automated testing of industrial automation software: practical receipts and lessons learned. In: Proceedings of the 1st International Workshop on Modern Software Engineering Methods for Industrial Automation - MoSEMInA 2014, pp. 7–16. ACM Press, Hyderabad, India (2014). http://dl.acm.org/citation.cfm?doid=2593783.2593788

11. Suresh, V.P., Chakrabarti, S., Jetley, R.: Automated test case generation for programmable logic controller code. In: Proceedings of the 12th Innovations on Software Engineering Conference (formerly known as India Software Engineering Conference) - ISEC 2019, pp. 1–4. ACM Press, Pune, India (2019). http://dl.acm.org/citation.cfm?doid=3299771.3299799

12. Pauker, F., Frühwirth, T., Kittl, B., Kastner, W.: A systematic approach to OPC UA information model design. Procedia CIRP **57**, 321–326 (2016). http://www.sciencedirect.com/science/article/pii/S2212827116312100

13. González, I., Calderón, A.J., Figueiredo, J., Sousa, J.M.C.: A literature survey on open platform communications (OPC) applied to advanced industrial environments. Electronics **8**(5), 510 (2019) https://www.mdpi.com/2079-9292/8/5/510

14. Klammer, C., Ramler, R.: A journey from manual testing to automated test generation in an industry project. In: 2017 IEEE International Conference on Software Quality, Reliability and Security Companion (QRS-C), pp. 591–592. IEEE, Prague, Czech Republic (2017). http://ieeexplore.ieee.org/document/8004387/

15. IEC 61131–3: Programmable controllers - Part 3: Programming languages. International Standard IEC 61131–3:2013, International Electrotechnical Commission, Geneva, CH (2013)

Quality Assurance for AI-Based Systems

Quality Assurance for AI-Based Systems: Overview and Challenges (Introduction to Interactive Session)

Michael Felderer[1](✉) and Rudolf Ramler[2]

[1] University of Innsbruck, Innsbruck, Austria
michael.felderer@uibk.ac.at
[2] Software Competence Center Hagenberg GmbH (SCCH),
Hagenberg im Mühlkreis, Austria
rudolf.ramler@scch.at

Abstract. The number and importance of AI-based systems in all domains is growing. With the pervasive use and the dependence on AI-based systems, the quality of these systems becomes essential for their practical usage. However, quality assurance for AI-based systems is an emerging area that has not been well explored and requires collaboration between the SE and AI research communities. This paper discusses terminology and challenges on quality assurance for AI-based systems to set a baseline for that purpose. Therefore, we define basic concepts and characterize AI-based systems along the three dimensions of artifact type, process, and quality characteristics. Furthermore, we elaborate on the key challenges of (1) understandability and interpretability of AI models, (2) lack of specifications and defined requirements, (3) need for validation data and test input generation, (4) defining expected outcomes as test oracles, (5) accuracy and correctness measures, (6) non-functional properties of AI-based systems, (7) self-adaptive and self-learning characteristics, and (8) dynamic and frequently changing environments.

Keywords: Artificial Intelligence · AI · AI-based systems · Machine learning · Software quality · System quality · AI quality · Quality assurance

1 Introduction

Recent advances in Artificial Intelligence (AI), especially in machine learning (ML) and deep learning (DL), and their integration into software-based systems of all domains raise new challenges to engineering modern AI-based systems. These systems are data-intensive, continuously evolving, self-adapting, and their behavior has a degree of (commonly accepted) uncertainty due to inherent non-determinism. These characteristics require adapted and new constructive and analytical quality assurance (QA) approaches from the field of software engineering (SE) in order to guarantee the quality during development and operation in

© Springer Nature Switzerland AG 2021
D. Winkler et al. (Eds.): SWQD 2021, LNBIP 404, pp. 33–42, 2021.
https://doi.org/10.1007/978-3-030-65854-0_3

live environments. However, as pointed out by Borg [1], already the concept of "quality" in AI-based systems is not well-defined. Furthermore, as pointed out by Lenarduzzi et al. [2], terminology differs in AI and software engineering.

The knowledge and background of different communities are brought together for developing AI-based systems. While this leads to new and innovative approaches, exciting breakthroughs, as well as a significant advancement in what can be achieved with modern AI-based systems, it also fuels the babel of terms, concepts, perceptions, and underlying assumptions and principles. For instance, the term "regression" in ML refers to regression models or regression analysis, whereas in SE it refers to regression testing. Speaking about "testing", this term is defined as the activity of executing the system to reveal defects in SE but refers to the evaluation of performance characteristics (e.g., accuracy) of a trained model with a holdout validation dataset in ML. The consequences are increasing confusion and potentially conflicting solutions for how to approach quality assurance for AI-based systems and how to tackle the associated challenges. While this paper starts from a software engineering point of view, its goal is to incorporate and discuss also many other perspectives, which eventually aggregate into a multi-dimensional big picture of quality assurance for AI-based systems.

In this paper, we first discuss the terminology on quality assurance for AI in Sect. 2. Then, we discuss challenges on QA for AI in Sect. 3. Finally, in Sect. 4 we conclude the paper.

2   Background and Terminology

AI-based system (also called *AI-enabled system*) refers to a software-based system that comprises AI components besides traditional software components. However, there are different definitions of what AI means, which vary in their scope and level of detail. AI is (human) intelligence demonstrated by machines, which implies the automation of tasks that normally would require human intelligence. For our context, i.e., quality assurance, we pragmatically include those AI techniques in our working definition of AI that require new or significantly adapted quality assurance techniques. This comprises supervised ML and DL, which require to transfer control from source code (where traditional QA can be applied) to data. Borg [1] explicitly introduces the term *MLware* for the subset of AI that, fueled by data, realizes functionality through machine learning.

Software quality is defined as the capability of a software product to satisfy stated and implied needs when used under specified conditions [3]. *Software quality assurance* is then the systematic examination of the extent to which a software product is capable of satisfying stated and implied needs [3].

AI components, especially based on supervised ML or DL, differ fundamentally from traditional components because they are data-driven in nature, i.e., their behavior is non-deterministic, statistics-orientated and evolves over time in response to the frequent provision of new data [4]. An AI component embedded in a system comprises the data, the ML model, and the framework. Data are collected and pre-processed for use. Learning program is the code for running to train the model. Framework (e.g., Weka, scikit-learn, and TensorFlow) offers algorithms and other libraries for developers to choose from when writing the learning program.

To characterize AI-based systems for the purpose of quality assurance, it is meaningful to consider several dimensions. Such dimensions are the *artifact type* dimension, the *process* dimension and the *quality characteristics* dimension. The dimensions and their values are shown in Fig. 1.

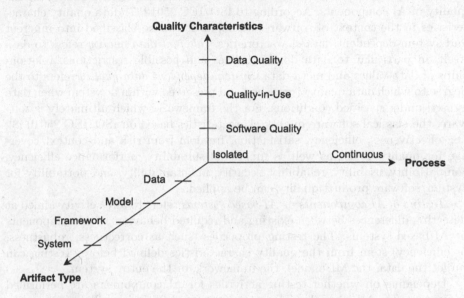

Fig. 1. Dimensions of AI-based systems and quality assurance

On the artifact type dimension, we can consider, based on the characterization of AI components in the previous paragraph, the system, framework, model and data perspective. On the process dimension, we can distinguish whether AI components and systems are developed in isolation or continuously by iteratively taking feedback from the deployed components into account based on DevOps principles. For all artifact and process settings, quality characteristics are relevant.

For instance, additional *quality properties* of AI components and AI-based systems have to be taken into account. Zhang et al. [5] consider the following quality properties:

- *Correctness* refers to the probability that an AI component gets things right.
- *Model relevance* measures how well an AI component fits the data.
- *Robustness* refers to the resilience of an AI component towards perturbations.
- *Security* measures the resilience against potential harm, danger or loss made via manipulating or illegally accessing AI components.
- *Data privacy* refers to the ability of an AI component to preserve private data information.

- *Efficiency* measures the construction or prediction speed of an AI component.
- *Fairness* ensures that decisions made by AI components are in the right way and for the right reason to avoid problems in human rights, discrimination, law, and other ethical issues.
- *Interpretability* refers to the degree to which an observer can understand the cause of a decision made by an AI component.

Felderer et al. [6] highlight the additional importance of *data quality* for the quality of AI components. According to ISO/IEC 25012 [7] data quality characteristics in the context of software development can be classified into inherent and system-dependent data characteristics. *Inherent data quality* refers to data itself, in particular to data domain values and possible restrictions, relationships of data values and meta-data. *System-dependent data quality* refers to the degree to which data quality is reached and preserved within a system when data is used under specified conditions. For the framework, which ultimately is software, the classical software quality characteristics based on ISO/IEC 25010 [8], i.e., effectiveness, efficiency, satisfaction, freedom from risk and context coverage for quality in use as well as functional suitability, performance efficiency, compatibility, usability, reliability, security, maintainability, and portability for system/software product quality can be applied.

Testing of AI components or *AI-based systems* refers to any activity aimed at detecting differences between existing and required behaviors of AI components or AI-based systems. The testing properties (such as correctness, robustness, or efficiency) stem from the quality characteristics defined before. Testing can target the data, the ML model, the framework, or the entire system.

Depending on whether testing activities for AI components are performed before or after ML model deployment one can distinguish offline and online testing. *Offline testing* tests the AI component with historical data, but not in an application environment [5]. Cross-validation using a validation dataset is a typical offline testing approach to make sure that the AI component meets the required conditions. *Online testing* tests deployed AI components in a real or virtual application environment. Online testing complements offline testing, because the latter relies on historical data not fully representing future data, is not able to test some problematic circumstances occurring in real environments like data loss, and has no access to direct user feedback. A common online testing technique is *A/B testing*, which is a splitting testing technique to compare two or more versions of a deployed component. A/B tests are often performed as experiments and the activity is called continuous experimentation in software engineering [9,10].

3   Challenges

A wide range of challenges exists, which stem from the novelty of the topic. Currently, there is a lack of (standardized) approaches for quality assurance of AI-based systems. Many attempts are in progress to fill the void. Yet the understanding of the problem is still very incomplete. It prolongs to fundamental questions like what are relevant quality characteristics (see previous section) and what is a bug. An example for a "new type of bug" unseen in conventional software is the phenomenon of adversarial examples [11], where small variations in the input (e.g., noise in image data or recorded speech that is not or barely noticeable for the human user) has a dramatic impact on the output as it results in a severe misclassification.

In addition to outlining important concepts and terms in the previous section, this section elaborates on the following key challenges encountered in the development of approaches for quality assurance and testing of AI-based systems.

- Understandability and interpretability of AI models
- Lack of specifications and defined requirements
- Need for validation data and test input generation
- Defining expected outcomes as test oracles
- Accuracy and correctness measures
- Non-functional properties of AI-based systems
- Self-adaptive and self-learning characteristics
- Dynamic and frequently changing environments.

Understandability and Interpretability: Data scientists are struggling with the problem that ML and in particular DL are producing models that are opaque, non-intuitive, and difficult for people to understand. The produced models turned out to be uninterpretable "black boxes" [12]. This challenge propagates to testing and quality assurance activities and it affects debugging models when they have confirmed defects. Black-box testing is a common approach in software quality assurance. So why does the lack of understandability and interpretability also have an impact on testing? The challenge for quality assurance results from the *lack of specifications and defined requirements* that developers and testers are used to have for conventional software systems and which provide the knowledge necessary to understand, build and test the system [13].

Lack of Specifications and Defined Requirements: Data-based/learning-based approaches do not rely on specifications and predefined requirements. They automatically generate models from existing data. The data used for learning consists of a wide range of input and labeled output. Model generation is an exploratory approach. Learning algorithms are applied to seek relevant "rules" how to connect the input to the expected output. Whether such rules can be found and how adequate they are to accurately model the connection is usually unclear at the beginning of the learning process.

Conventional software development works in the exact opposite way compared to data-based/learning-based approaches [14]. Specifications are defining the required behavior of the system, i.e., the "rules". They are available before the system is implemented. People have learned about relevant rules, for example, by experience (e.g., domain experts) or because they have acquired the knowledge from specifications (e.g., developers). The goal in testing conventionally developed systems is to come up with inputs and labeled outputs to verify and validate the implemented rules. Testing explores representative scenarios as well as boundaries and corner cases. This goal is also important for testing AI-based systems. However, testing techniques for conventional systems are supposed to rely on specifications to derive inputs or to determine the expected outcome for an input, which leads to further challenges such as the challenge of *test input generation* and *defining test oracles* when testing AI-based systems.

Test Input Generation: In testing, it is usually the case that systems have a huge input space to be explored. Hence, at the core of any testing approach is the problem that completely exercising even a moderately complex system is impossible due to the combinatorial explosion of the number of possible inputs. Testing AI-based systems is no difference [15].

Software testing techniques commonly deal with the challenge of huge input spaces by adopting sampling strategies for selecting inputs when designing test cases. A number of testing techniques have been developed that are classified [16] as specification-based (black-box), structure-based (white-box), or experience-based. Similar techniques suitable for AI-based system testing are yet to emerge. First techniques have been proposed that exploit structure information of deep neural networks to derive coverage measures such as various forms of neuron coverage (see, e.g., [17]). Inputs (test data) is generated with the goal to maximize coverage. Various approaches are currently explored, from random generation (fuzzing) [17] to GAN-based metamorphic approaches [18]. However, due to the lack of interpretability and understandability (resulting from a lack of specifications and requirements), identifying and selecting representative inputs to construct meaningful test cases is still an open challenge [19].

Defining Test Oracles: The goal of testing is to reveal faults in terms of incorrect responses or behavior of the system in reaction to a specific input. In order to determine whether the observed output (responses and behavior) is correct or incorrect, it has to be compared to some expected output. The source providing information about what is a correct output is called test oracle [20]. In manually constructing test cases, a human tester defines the input and the corresponding expected output. In a production setting, however, the input is dynamically created throughout the actual use of the system in a particular context or environment. It typically includes values and value combinations that have never been used before and which were even not anticipated to be used at all. Hence, the "oracle problem" of determining the correct output for an input, a core challenge in testing, dramatically increases when testing in performed in production environments under diverse settings.

Accuracy and Correctness: Closely related is the *accuracy problem*. Software is expected to be deterministic and correct. Any deviation from the expected behavior and any difference in the output is considered a defect that is supposed to be fixed. It is well known, that real-world software is not defect-free and there is no perfect system. However, the underlying principles and the level of correctness currently achieved in software engineering is different from what AI-based systems exhibit. AI-based systems are accepted to be inherently "defective", as they usually operate in a defined accuracy range. Yet a system with 99% accuracy will "fail" in about one out of hundred runs. Applying conventional testing and quality assurance principles and approaches is incompatible with the underlying assumption that the system is considered correct although it exhibits a high number of contradicting ("failing") cases. The corresponding testing techniques and quality metrics developed for deterministic systems first need to be adapted before they can be used to assess systems with probabilistic behavior.

Non-functional Properties: Testing for *non-functional aspects* is always challenging and requires suitable approaches to specify expected properties. This also holds for testing of AI-based systems, where testing non-functional aspects has rarely been explored [5]. Especially robustness and efficiency are well suited for testing in production. Testing robustness of AI components is challenging because input data has more diverse forms, for instance image or audio data. Especially adversarial robustness, where perturbations are designed to be hard to detect are also hard to define in terms of corresponding test oracles. Metamorphic relations [21,22] are therefore frequently exploited as alternative ways to construct test oracles. Testing efficiency for AI components has to deal not only with prediction speed, but also with construction speed, which poses challenges to measuring and analyzing performance, especially in a real-time context when decisions have to be made instantaneous (e.g., in autonomous driving).

Self-adaptive and Self-learning Systems: Regression testing is a major task in any modern software development project. The agile paradigm and the DevOps movement have led to short development cycles with frequent releases as well as the widespread use of techniques such as Continuous Integration, Deployment, and Delivery [23]. The answer to the question how quality assurance can keep up with the continuously growing development speed is automated testing. Test automation, however, is a major cost-driver. First, due to the effort for initially setting up the test environment and implementing the automated tests, and second, even more so due to the effort for maintaining the automated tests when the system under test has been changed [24]. In contrast to conventional software that is evolved over a series of development iterations, many AI-based systems are designed to evolve dynamically at run-time by self-adapting to changing environments and continuously learning from the input they process [25]. Testing dynamic self-adaptive systems raises many open issues about how to cope with the complexity and dynamics that result from the flexibility of self-adaptive and self-learning systems [26].

Dynamic Environments: AI components often operate in dynamic and frequently changing environments. Examples are typically data intensive applications that have to integrate data from various sources (including sensors, web data, etc.), which all have different characteristics regarding their data quality [27,28]. Data can also stem from simulators or AI components may have to control simulations. Due to the complexity and non-determinism of the environment, testability (i.e., controllability and observability) is highly challenging. Furthermore, due to information heterogeneity also privacy and security aspects are essential. To address these issues, run-time monitoring and online testing have been suggested. Online testing, the assessment of the system's behavior is performed live, in production and in a real application environment [5].

Real application environments provide the advantage of real user integration and real user experience. In modern cloud-based environments user information can easily be collected and used to evaluate and continuously improve the system (e.g., in web-based recommender systems). However, this requires a significant number of users with a clear user profile. In addition, applying testing in production for business-critical users poses business risks. In addition, one has to carefully select metrics to guarantee their validity and reliability. The term "testing in production" can even be considered as an oxymoron, especially if systems are safety-critical and can harm the health of impacted stakeholders (e.g., for autonomous systems controlling vehicles). In that context, clear constraints have to be defined and guarantees under which conditions testing in production can be performed at all because safety-criticality requires clear strategies to remove defects before deployment or to handle them properly in production. However, besides safety also privacy and ethical issues may restrict the applicability of testing in production and therefore require specific constraints and monitors.

4   Summary and Conclusions

In this paper, we discussed terminology and challenges on quality assurance for AI-based systems. To characterize AI-based systems for the purpose of quality assurance, we defined the three dimensions artifact type (i.e., data, model, framework, and system), process (from isolated to continuous), and quality characteristics (with respect to software quality, quality-in-use, and data quality). Furthermore, we elaborated on the key challenges of (1) understandability and interpretability of AI models, (2) lack of specifications and defined requirements, (3) need for validation data and test input generation, (4) defining expected outcomes as test oracles, (5) accuracy and correctness measures, (6) non-functional properties of AI-based systems, (7) self-adaptive and self-learning characteristics, and (8) dynamic and frequently changing environments.

In order to properly address the challenges raised in this paper and to enable high quality AI-based systems, first and foremost, exchange of knowledge and ideas between the SE and the AI community is needed. One channel of exchange is education or training through dedicated courses [29] or media [30]. Another one are dedicated venues for exchange and discussion of challenges on quality assurance for AI-based systems like the IEEE International Conference On Artificial Intelligence Testing or the workshop Quality Assurance for AI collocated with the Software Quality Days.

Acknowledgments. The research reported in this paper has been partly funded by the Federal Ministry for Climate Action, Environment, Energy, Mobility, Innovation and Technology (BMK), the Federal Ministry for Digital and Economic Affairs (BMDW), and the Province of Upper Austria in the frame of the COMET - Competence Centers for Excellent Technologies Programme managed by Austrian Research Promotion Agency FFG.

References

1. Borg, M.: The AIQ meta-testbed: pragmatically bridging academic AI testing and industrial Q needs. In: SWQD 2021. LNBIP, vol. 404, pp. 66–77. Springer, Cham (2021)
2. Lenarduzzi, V., Lomio, F., Moreschini, S., Taibi, D., Tamburri, D.A.: Software quality for AI: where we are now? In: SWQD 2021. LNBIP, vol. 404, pp. 43–53. Springer, Cham (2021)
3. ISO/IEC: ISO/IEC 25000:2005 software engineering—software product quality requirements and evaluation (square)—guide to square. Technical report, ISO (2011)
4. Amershi, S., et al.: Software engineering for machine learning: a case study. In: 2019 IEEE/ACM 41st International Conference on Software Engineering: Software Engineering in Practice (ICSE-SEIP), pp. 291–300. IEEE (2019)
5. Zhang, J.M., Harman, M., Ma, L., Liu, Y.: Machine learning testing: survey, landscapes and horizons. IEEE Trans. Softw. Eng. **PP**, 1 (2020)
6. Felderer, M., Russo, B., Auer, F.: On testing data-intensive software systems. In: Biffl, S., Eckhart, M., Lüder, A., Weippl, E. (eds.) Security and Quality in Cyber-Physical Systems Engineering, pp. 129–148. Springer, Cham (2019). https://doi.org/10.1007/978-3-030-25312-7_6
7. ISO/IEC: ISO/IEC 25012:2008 software engineering – software product quality requirements and evaluation (square) – data quality model. Technical report, ISO (2008)
8. ISO/IEC: ISO/IEC 25010:2011 systems and software engineering – systems and software quality requirements and evaluation (square) – system and software quality models. Technical report, ISO (2011)
9. Ros, R., Runeson, P.: Continuous experimentation and A/B testing: a mapping study. In: 2018 IEEE/ACM 4th International Workshop on Rapid Continuous Software Engineering (RCoSE), pp. 35–41. IEEE (2018)
10. Auer, F., Felderer, M.: Current state of research on continuous experimentation: a systematic mapping study. In: 2018 44th Euromicro Conference on Software Engineering and Advanced Applications (SEAA), pp. 335–344. IEEE (2018)
11. Yuan, X., He, P., Zhu, Q., Li, X.: Adversarial examples: attacks and defenses for deep learning. IEEE Trans. Neural Netw. Learn. Syst. **30**(9), 2805–2824 (2019)
12. Goebel, R., et al.: Explainable AI: the new 42? In: Holzinger, A., Kieseberg, P., Tjoa, A.M., Weippl, E. (eds.) CD-MAKE 2018. LNCS, vol. 11015, pp. 295–303. Springer, Cham (2018). https://doi.org/10.1007/978-3-319-99740-7_21
13. Bosch, J., Olsson, H.H., Crnkovic, I.: It takes three to tango: requirement, outcome/data, and AI driven development. In: SiBW, pp. 177–192 (2018)
14. Fischer, L., et al.: Applying AI in practice: key challenges and lessons learned. In: Holzinger, A., Kieseberg, P., Tjoa, A.M., Weippl, E. (eds.) CD-MAKE 2020. LNCS, vol. 12279, pp. 451–471. Springer, Cham (2020). https://doi.org/10.1007/978-3-030-57321-8_25
15. Marijan, D., Gotlieb, A., Ahuja, M.K.: Challenges of testing machine learning based systems. In: 2019 IEEE International Conference On Artificial Intelligence Testing (AITest), pp. 101–102. IEEE (2019)
16. ISO/IEC/IEEE international standard - software and systems engineering—software testing–part 4: Test techniques, pp. 1–149. ISO/IEC/IEEE 29119-4:2015 (2015)

17. Xie, X., et al.: DeepHunter: a coverage-guided fuzz testing framework for deep neural networks. In: Proceedings of the 28th ACM SIGSOFT International Symposium on Software Testing and Analysis, ISSTA 2019, pp. 146–157. Association for Computing Machinery, New York (2019)

18. Zhang, M., Zhang, Y., Zhang, L., Liu, C., Khurshid, S.: DeepRoad: GAN-based metamorphic testing and input validation framework for autonomous driving systems. In: 2018 33rd IEEE/ACM International Conference on Automated Software Engineering (ASE), pp. 132–142. IEEE (2018)

19. Braiek, H.B., Khomh, F.: On testing machine learning programs. J. Syst. Softw. **164**, 110542 (2020)

20. Barr, E.T., Harman, M., McMinn, P., Shahbaz, M., Yoo, S.: The Oracle problem in software testing: a survey. IEEE Trans. Softw. Eng. **41**(5), 507–525 (2015)

21. Xie, X., Ho, J.W., Murphy, C., Kaiser, G., Xu, B., Chen, T.Y.: Testing and validating machine learning classifiers by metamorphic testing. J. Syst. Softw. **84**(4), 544–558 (2011)

22. Dwarakanath, A., et al.: Identifying implementation bugs in machine learning based image classifiers using metamorphic testing. In: Proceedings of the 27th ACM SIGSOFT International Symposium on Software Testing and Analysis, pp. 118–128 (2018)

23. Humble, J., Farley, D.: Continuous Delivery: Reliable Software Releases through Build, Test, and Deployment Automation. Pearson Education, London (2010)

24. Garousi, V., Felderer, M.: Developing, verifying, and maintaining high-quality automated test scripts. IEEE Softw. **33**(3), 68–75 (2016)

25. Khritankov, A.: On feedback loops in lifelong machine learning systems. In: SWQD 2021. LNBIP, vol. 404, pp. 54–65. Springer, Cham (2021)

26. Eberhardinger, B., Seebach, H., Knapp, A., Reif, W.: Towards testing self-organizing, adaptive systems. In: Merayo, M.G., de Oca, E.M. (eds.) ICTSS 2014. LNCS, vol. 8763, pp. 180–185. Springer, Heidelberg (2014). https://doi.org/10.1007/978-3-662-44857-1_13

27. Foidl, H., Felderer, M., Biffl, S.: Technical debt in data-intensive software systems. In: 2019 45th Euromicro Conference on Software Engineering and Advanced Applications (SEAA), pp. 338–341. IEEE (2019)

28. Foidl, H., Felderer, M.: Risk-based data validation in machine learning-based software systems. In: Proceedings of the 3rd ACM SIGSOFT International Workshop on Machine Learning Techniques for Software Quality Evaluation, pp. 13–18 (2019)

29. Kästner, C., Kang, E.: Teaching software engineering for AI-enabled systems. arXiv preprint arXiv:2001.06691 (2020)

30. Hulten, G.: Building Intelligent Systems. Springer, Berkeley (2018). https://doi.org/10.1007/978-1-4842-3432-7

Software Quality for AI: Where We Are Now?

Valentina Lenarduzzi[1](✉), Francesco Lomio[2], Sergio Moreschini[2],
Davide Taibi[2], and Damian Andrew Tamburri[3]

[1] LUT University, Lahti, Finland
valentina.lenarduzzi@lut.fi
[2] Tampere University, Tampere, Finland
{francesco.lomio,sergio.moreschini,davide.taibi}@tuni.fi
[3] Eindhoven University of Technology - JADS, 's-Hertogenbosch, The Netherlands
d.a.tamburri@tue.nl

Abstract. Artificial Intelligence is getting more and more popular,
being adopted in a large number of applications and technology we use
on a daily basis. However, a large number of Artificial Intelligence applications are produced by developers without proper training on software
quality practices or processes, and in general, lack in-depth knowledge
regarding software engineering processes. The main reason is due to the
fact that the machine-learning engineer profession has been born very
recently, and currently there is a very limited number of training or
guidelines on issues (such as code quality or testing) for machine learning and applications using machine learning code. In this work, we aim
at highlighting the main software quality issues of Artificial Intelligence
systems, with a central focus on machine learning code, based on the
experience of our four research groups. Moreover, we aim at defining a
shared research road map, that we would like to discuss and to follow
in collaboration with the workshop participants. As a result, the software quality of AI-enabled systems is often poorly tested and of very
low quality.

Keywords: Software quality · AI software

1 Introduction

The term Artificial Intelligence (AI) commonly indicates a software system that
is capable of mimicking human intelligence [27]. AI systems are capable of performing actions thanks to underlying algorithms that can learn from the data
without being specifically programmed. The set of these algorithms are referred
to as Machine Learning (ML) algorithms [21].

As any software system, AI systems require attention attaining quality assurance, and in particular to their code quality [26]. Conversely, current development processes, and in particular agile models, enable companies to decide the

© Springer Nature Switzerland AG 2021
D. Winkler et al. (Eds.): SWQD 2021, LNBIP 404, pp. 43–53, 2021.
https://doi.org/10.1007/978-3-030-65854-0_4

technologies to adopt in their system in a later stage and it becomes hard to anticipate if a system, or if a data pipeline is used for Machine-Learning (ML) produces high-quality models [23].

The need for considering the quality of AI-enabled systems was highlighted already even more than 30 years ago [26,31]. For the time being, different approaches have been proposed to evaluate the quality of the AI-models but little in the way of AI code quality itself (e.g. [15] and [8]).

Conversely, as already mentioned, the overall quality of the AI-enabled systems, and in particular the ML code has never been investigated systematically so far if not anecdotally. For example, a report from Informatics Europe[1] and the ACM Europe Council[2], as well as the Networked European Software and Services Initiative[3], highlighted the importance of assessing the quality of AI-related code [16,23]. The EU has also proposed a whitepaper discussing a high-level approach to the regulatory compliance of AI, but did not focus on code quality issues at all [12].

AI code needs to be maintained. Therefore, developers need to take care of the quality of their code, and keep the technical debt [6] under control [28].

The goal of this paper is to highlight the quality-related issues of AI software, as well as possible solutions that can be adopted to solve them. The identification of such quality issues is based on the experience of our four research groups: (1) the Software Engineering group of the LUT University, (2) the Machine Learning and (3) Software Engineering groups of the Tampere University, and the (4) Jheronimus Academy Data and Engineering (JADE) lab of the Jheronimus Academy of Data Science.

The insights in this paper enable researchers to understand possible problems on the quality of AI-enabled systems opening new research topics and allows companies to understand how to better address quality issues in their systems.

The remainder of this paper is structured as follows. Section 2 presents Related works. Section 3 described the current issues on code quality of AI-enabled systems, Sect. 4 proposes our shared road map while Sect. 5 draws conclusions.

2   Related Work

As any software system, AI-enabled software, and in general ML code, require to pay attention to quality assurance, and in particular to the code quality. Current development processes, and in particular agile models, enable companies to decide the technologies to adopt in their system in a later stage. Therefore, it is hard to anticipate if a system, or if a data pipeline used for ML will produce high-quality models [23].

---

[1] Informatics Europe https://www.informatics-europe.org.

[2] ACM Europe Council https://europe.acm.org.

[3] The Networked European Software and Services Initiative - NESSI http://www.nessi-europe.com.

A limited number of peer-reviewed works highlighted the quality issue in AI-enabled software.

Murphy et al. [22] proposed a testing framework for Machine Learning (ML), introducing the concept of regression testing and an approach for ranking the correctness of new versions of ML algorithms. Besides the proposed model, they also highlighted conflicting technical terms with very different meanings to machine learning experts than they do to software engineers (e.g. "testing", "regression", "validation", "model"). Moreover, they raised the problem of code quality, reporting that future works should address it. Related to the matter of ML testing, Zhang et al. provided a comprehensive survey research [30]. In this work with the term ML testing, they refer to *"any activity aimed at detecting differences between existing and required behaviors of machine learning systems."* The work comprehends a section related to fundamental terminology in ML which will be referred to in Table 1.

Nakajima, in his invited talk, call the attention the product quality of ML-based systems, identifying new challenges for quality assurance methods. He proposed to identify new testing methods for ML-based systems, proposing to adopt Metamorphic testing [10] is a pseudo oracle approach and uses golden outputs as testing values.

Pimentel et al. [10] investigated the reproducibility of Jupyter notebooks, showing that less than 50% of notebooks are reproducible, opening new questions to our community to propose advanced approaches for analyzing Jupyter notebooks. Wang et al. [29] analyzed 2.5 Million of Jupiter notebooks investigating their code quality reporting that notebooks are inundated with poor quality code, e.g., not respecting recommended coding practices, or containing unused variables and deprecated functions. They also report that poor coding practices, as well as the lack of quality control, might be propagated into the next generation of developers. Hence, they argue that there is a strong need to identify quality practices, but especially a quality culture in the ML community.

The vast majority of grey literature also focuses on the quality of the ML models or on the data. Only a limited number of authors raised the problem of the overall product quality or of the quality of the ML code. Vignesh [24] proposed to continuously validate the quality of ML models considering black boxes techniques and evaluating the performance of model post-deployment on test data sets and new data from production scenarios. He also proposes to adopt metamorphic testing, involving data mutation to augment test data sets used for evaluating model performance and accuracy.

It is interesting to note that Vignesh recommends exposing models being tested as RESTful service, instead of testing internally or manually. As for the quality of the code of ML Models, Dhaval [20] proposes to introduce code review processes for ML developers, adopting code reviewing techniques traditionally adopted in SW Engineering.

Besides the model itself, the essence of a good machine learning-based software relies on the data used to train the network. It is therefore vital to take into account the characteristics and features that mark a specific application and meet such qualities in the data used to develop it. Hence, some of the requirements that the data needs to meet are: context compatibility, incorruptibility, and completeness. In a data-driven software scenario, it is not rare to find to encounter a situation in which the same data set is used to train networks with different goals. As an example, most of the networks generated in computer vision are fine-tuned over a first tuning on ImageNET [13]. In such a situation it is very important to take into account the *compatibility* between the context for which the data has been created and the one we are trying to use the data for. With *incorruptibility* we define the quality of a data set to be resistant to external factors that might generate errors, or undesired changes, during writing, reading, storage, transmission, or processing.

A data set is *complete*, related to a specific application when it is capable of describing and defining specific information (in the form of mono or multidimensional variables) in its entirety. Related to a Machine Learning-based approach we say that the data set is complete when it is capable of tuning the weights to generate the desired result without any requirement for fine-tuning. As an example, we take the MNIST data set [17] which is complete if we are training a network to understand handwritten digits, but not in the case when we want to train a network to understand handwriting as it does not include letters. To this matter, an ulterior data set has been created, known as EMNIST [11].

Lwakatare et al. performed the work closest to this work [19]. They discussed software engineering challenges based on a survey conducted on four companies. The result is a taxonomy of challenges that consider the life-cycle activities of ML code (such as assemble data set, create model, (re)train and evaluate, deploy). However, differently than in our work, they did not identify clear issues and possible solutions.

3   AI Software Quality: Key Issues and Comments

Based on the collective experience of our groups and through simple self-ethnography [9], we elicited different code quality issues commonly faced by all sorts of stakeholders (e.g., our research assistant working for consultancy projects in AI, our colleagues, and our students as developers of AI Software) working with AI software. In this Section, we describe the aforementioned elicitation, also discussing possible solutions that might be adopted to solve the emerged issues.

– **Developers Skills and Training.** Once the suitable data has been chosen and proven to be compliant with our requirements the next step involves coding. The machine learning engineer profession was born less than a decade ago and therefore, no training guidelines have been outlined yet. Most of the professionals that occupy this position have been moving from a similar field such as mathematics, physics, or computer vision. This grouping of different backgrounds generated "communication problems" which reflected in the way the code was written. We identify four open problems nested in this macro area: code understandability, code quality guidelines, training problems, and the absence of tools for software quality improvement. One of the main issues of AI Developers is the lack of skills in software engineering, and especially the lack of skills in software quality and maintenance. The reason is that AI developers are often experts borrowed from other fields such as physics or mathematics. The lack of skills in software quality is then reflected in their code. Moreover, as highlighted by Wang et al. [29], the AI code examples often provided online by AI experts and teachers are of low quality, mainly because they lack in software engineering skills. As a result, these poor coding practices may further be propagated into the next generation of developers. For these reasons, there has been a rise in the number of courses created to instruct specific approaches related to AI in different fields [14].

– **Development Processes.** Because of the aforementioned lack of skills and training in software engineering, AI developers often lack knowledge of development processes. As a result, in our experience, it is often hard to introduce them into running agile processes, while it is much easier to introduce them into a waterfall process. The main reason is their problem in segmenting the work into smaller units or user stories, and to incrementally deliver the results, as usually done in agile processes.

– **Testing Processes.** Testing AI code is usually considered for AI developers as testing and training the machine learning algorithms. The introduction of unit and integration testing is of paramount importance to ensure the correct execution of software systems. However, the different testing practices, usually applied in software engineering, are not commonly applied to the AI-related code, but only to the overall systems including them, and the AI-specific function is not commonly part of the CI/CD pipeline. The reason might be in the complexity of running tests, and the problem of the non-deterministic results of the AI-algorithms. Metamorphic testing can be a good solution, at least to run unit testing.

– **Deployment confidence.** Developers commonly prefer to manually test their AI-models, and then to manually deploy the systems in production, mainly because they are not confident in releasing every change automatically. The reason is still connected to the lack of clear testing processes and the last of integration of unit and integration tests.

– **Code Quality.** AI-code is often of very low quality, mainly because of the lack of quality guidelines, quality checks, and standards. We might expect the IDEs to highlight possible "code smells" in the code, or to highlight possible styling issues. However, the current support from IDEs is very limited.

Specific libraries, such as Tensorflow, refer to the document PEP-8 [25], which is the official style guide for Python code. However, the latter does not take into account the specific pipeline which involves the different stages of developing AI-code. An interesting initiative is conducted by Pytorch, which relies on Pytorch [4], a wrapper developed to organize the code in sections and separates the research code (dataloader, optimizer, training step) from the engineering code (i.e. training process). Even if Pytorch does not provide clear styling guidelines, it pushes developers to adopt clear guidelines for structuring the code.

- **Incompatibility of new version of ML libraries.** A well known problem in ML, is the necessity of installing a specific version of libraries as most of those might not be compatible with their future releases mining the success of the final project. This often creates inconsistency and incompatibility of the old version of the system with newer versions [1,2,5]. A possible workaround is to use microservices, adopting a specific version of a library on a service, and eventually another version of the same library on another service. However, when the existing code needs to be executed on a newer version of the same library, migration issues need to be considered.
- **Code Portability.** The rise of multiple libraries for ML training together with the different background of the engineers generated a new *"Babel tower"* for coding. Libraries such as Pytorch or Tensorflow have a different backbone which makes the same application look very different from one another. Therefore, to understand and port the code from one library to the other, it is often nontrivial.
- **Terminology.** AI and Software Engineering usually adopts the same terms for different purposes. This issue usually creates misunderstandings between developers with different backgrounds. In order to clarify the terms adopted by both domain, in Table 1 we present and describe the most common misleading terms together with their meaning in AI and in SW Engineering. Some terms have a totally different meaning in the two domains, while others might be used for the same purpose in different contexts. As an example, the term "parameter", besides the different definitions proposed in Table 1, is in both cases used to describe inputs or properties of objects for configuration. As another example, the term "code" can be also used in AI to describe the set of instructions to build the different layers, to recall the input dataset, and to perform training, test (and when necessary validation).
- **Communication between AI Developers and other developers.** Because of the different terminology adopted, we commonly experienced communication challenges between AI and other developers. As an example, we often had communication issues with AI developers without a software engineering background, especially when discussing scalability, architectural, or development processes related issues.

4   Research Roadmap

In order to address the issues reported in Sect. 3, we would like to share a collaborative research road map, that we are aiming at investigating in collaboration with different groups.

- Identify the most common quality issues in AI code using traditional SW Engineering methodologies. In this step, we are aiming at conducting a set of empirical studies among AI-developers and end-users of AI-based systems, intending to elicit the most important internal quality issues experienced by the developers and the external issues perceived by the users of the same systems.

Table 1. The terminology adopted in AI and in SW engineering

Term	Machine learning	Software engineering
Class	"One of a set of enumerated target value for a label" resulted from a classification model [3]	An extensible template definition for instantiating objects in object-oriented programming
Code	The possible values of a field (variable), also known as "category"	The source code
Distribution	Probability distribution (from statistics). Sometimes also referred to distributed computing or parallelism	Distributed computing. In testing, refers to the testing of distributed systems
Example	An entry from a dataset, composed of at least one features and a label, that can be used in model training and/or after training during inference. (also known as Observation)	An example system or piece of software often found in software documentation
Execution Environment	The set of all the libraries which are installed, and lately imported in the compiler. Specifically, in reinforcement learning, is the observable world exposed to a learning agent [3]	A system comprised of hardware and software tools used by the developers to build/deploy software
Feature	A characterizing variable found in the input data to a machine learning model. Predictions about the data can be made after gaining insight from these features (training)	A distinguishing characteristic of a software item
Function	A mathematical function, mapping parameters to a domain	In principle the same, in practice refers to the implementation in the source code
Label	In supervised learning: expected output for a training case. For example, an email message may be labeled as SPAM or non-SPAM [3]	A label refers to the name of a text field in a form or user interface (e.g the label of a button)
Layer	A set of neurons in a neural network that operates on input data (possibly from previous layers) and provides inputs to the next layer(s) as their outputs [3]	A layer in a multilayered software solution, e.g. data access layer, business logic layer, presentation layer
Model	Output of a ML algorithm after it has been trained from the training data, the learning program, and frameworks [30]	Different meaning, depending on the context: Development Model (process), Data Model (Database schema), ...
Network	Usually assuming Neural Network	Usually assuming Computer Network

(*continued*)

Table 1. (*continued*)

Term	Machine learning	Software engineering
Parameter	A variable in a model that is adjusted during training to minimize loss. E.g. weights or normalization parameters	A variable that holds a piece of data provided to a function as an input argument
Pattern	Detecting patterns in a dataset	Design patterns or architectural patterns
Performance	How well a certain model performs according to the selected metrics, e.g. precision, recall, or false positives, after training [21]	How fast a certain piece of software executes and/or how efficient it is
Quality	See performance	Software quality, including internal (e.g. code quality) and external quality (e.g. usability, performance, ...)
Reference	The baseline category used to compare with other categories	The variable that points to a memory address of another variable
Regression	Estimate numerical values, identifying relationships, and correlations between different types of data [30]	Regression (Testing) is a full or partial selection of already executed test cases which are re-executed to ensure that a recent program or code change has not adversely affected existing features
Testing	The process of evaluating a network over a set of data which has not been used for training and/or validation	Check whether the actual results match the expected results and to ensure that the software system is Defect free
Training	The process of tuning the weights and biased of a network recursively by making use of labeled examples	Developer's training
Validation	The process of using data outside the training set, known as the validation set, to evaluate the model quality. Important to ensure the generalization of the model outside the training set [3]	Verification and validation is the process of checking that a software system meets specifications and that it fulfills its intended purpose (requirements)

- Identify a set of testing techniques applicable to AI-enabled systems, to allow their execution into the CI/CD pipeline, and increase their confidence in the deployment.

- Identify a set of quality rules for the code and develop a linter for detecting code-level issues for the most common libraries and languages, starting from widely used tools for static code analysis [18] and technical debt analysis [7].
- Integrate into our master courses of Machine Learning a course on software engineering, with a special focus on the maintenance and testing of the AI-enabled applications.

5 Conclusion

In this work, we highlighted the most common quality issues that our developers face during the development of AI-enabled systems, based on the experience of our three research groups.

Overall, the training of developers is one of the biggest lacks in AI, which usually brings several issues related to low code quality of AI-code as well as low long-term maintenance.

Acknowledgement. We would like to thank the software engineering and AI community and in particular Taher Ahmed Ghaleb, Steffen Herbold, Idan Huji, Marcos Kalinowski, Christian Kästner, Janet Siegmund and Daniel Strüber for helping us on the definition of the glossary of AI and SW Engineering terms[4].

References

1. TensorFlow version compatibility. https://www.tensorflow.org/guide/versions
2. Compatible Versions of PyTorch/Libtorch with Cuda 10.0 (2019). https://discuss. pytorch.org/t/compatible-versions-of-pytorch-libtorch-with-cuda-10-0/58506. Accessed 11 July 2020
3. Machine Learning Glossary, Google Developers (2019). https://developers.google. com/machine-learning/glossary. Accessed 28 Aug 2020
4. Pytorch Lightning. The lightweight PyTorch wrapper for ML researchers (2019). https://github.com/PyTorchLightning/pytorch-lightning. Accessed 11 July 2020
5. Tensorflow 1.11.0 incompatible with keras2.2.2? (2019). https://github.com/ tensorflow/tensorflow/issues/22601. Accessed 11 July 2020
6. Avgeriou, P., Kruchten, P., Ozkaya, I., Seaman, C.: Managing technical debt in software engineering (Dagstuhl seminar 16162). Dagstuhl Reports 6 (2016)
7. Avgeriou, P., et al.: An overview and comparison of technical debt measurement tools. IEEE Softw. (2021)
8. Bradley, A.P.: The use of the area under the ROC curve in the evaluation of machine learning algorithms. Pattern Recogn. **30**(7), 1145–1159 (1997)
9. Britten, N., Campbell, R., Pope, C., Donovan, J., Morgan, M., Pill, R.: Using meta ethnography to synthesise qualitative research: a worked example. J. Health Serv. Res. Policy **7**(4), 209–215 (2002). http://www.ncbi.nlm.nih.gov/pubmed/12425780
10. Chen, T.Y.: Metamorphic testing: a simple method for alleviating the test oracle problem. In: Proceedings of the 10th International Workshop on Automation of Software Test, AST 2015, pp. 53–54. IEEE Press (2015)

---

[4] https://twitter.com/vale_lenarduzzi/status/1295055334264975360. Last access: 28 August 2020.

11. Cohen, G., Afshar, S., Tapson, J., Van Schaik, A.: EMNIST: extending MNIST to handwritten letters. In: 2017 International Joint Conference on Neural Networks (IJCNN), pp. 2921–2926. IEEE (2017)

12. Commission, E.: WHITE PAPER On Artificial Intelligence - A European approach to excellence and trust (2020). https://ec.europa.eu/info/sites/info/files/commission-white-paper-artificial-intelligence-feb2020_en.pdf?utm_source=CleverReach&utm_medium=email&utm_campaign=23-02-2020+Instituts-Journal+07%2F20%3A+Wo+waren+Sie%3F+Es+ging+um+Sie%21&utm_content=Mailing_11823061. Accessed 09 July 2020

13. Deng, J., Dong, W., Socher, R., Li, L.J., Li, K., Fei-Fei, L.: ImageNet: a large-scale hierarchical image database. In: 2009 IEEE Conference on Computer Vision and Pattern Recognition, pp. 248–255. IEEE (2009)

14. Kästner, C., Kang, E.: Teaching software engineering for AI-enabled systems. arXiv preprint arXiv:2001.06691 (2020)

15. Kohavi, R.: A study of cross-validation and bootstrap for accuracy estimation and model selection. In: Proceedings of the 14th International Joint Conference on Artificial Intelligence, IJCAI 1995, vol. 2, pp. 1137–1143. Morgan Kaufmann Publishers Inc., San Francisco (1995)

16. Larus, J., et al.: When computers decide: European recommendations on machine-learned automated decision making (2018)

17. LeCun, Y., Bottou, L., Bengio, Y., Haffner, P.: Gradient-based learning applied to document recognition. Proc. IEEE 86(11), 2278–2324 (1998)

18. Lenarduzzi, V., Sillitti, A., Taibi, D.: A survey on code analysis tools for software maintenance prediction. In: Ciancarini, P., Mazzara, M., Messina, A., Sillitti, A., Succi, G. (eds.) SEDA 2018. AISC, vol. 925, pp. 165–175. Springer, Cham (2020). https://doi.org/10.1007/978-3-030-14687-0_15

19. Lwakatare, L.E., Raj, A., Bosch, J., Olsson, H.H., Crnkovic, I.: A taxonomy of software engineering challenges for machine learning systems: an empirical investigation. In: Kruchten, P., Fraser, S., Coallier, F. (eds.) XP 2019. LNBIP, vol. 355, pp. 227–243. Springer, Cham (2019). https://doi.org/10.1007/978-3-030-19034-7_14

20. Dhaval, M.: How to perform Quality Assurance for Machine Learning models? (2018). https://medium.com/datadriveninvestor/how-to-perform-quality-assurance-for-ml-models-cef77bbbcfb. Accessed 09 July 2020

21. Mitchell, T.M.: Machine Learning. McGraw-Hill, New York (2010). [u.a.]. http://www.amazon.com/Machine-Learning-Tom-M-Mitchell/dp/0070428077

22. Murphy, C., Kaiser, G.E., Arias, M.: A framework for quality assurance of machine learning applications. Columbia University Computer Science Technical reports, CUCS-034-06 (2006)

23. NESSI: Software and Artificial Intelligence (2019). http://www.nessi-europe.com/files/NESSI%20-%20Software%20and%20AI%20-%20issue%201.pdf. Accessed 09 July 2020

24. Radhakrishnan, V.: How to perform Quality Assurance for Machine Learning models? (2019). https://blog.sasken.com/quality-assurance-for-machine-learning-models-part-1-why-quality-assurance-is-critical-for-machine-learning-models. Accessed 09 July 2020

25. van Rossum, G., Warsaw, B., Coghlan, N.: PEP 8 - Style Guide for Python Code. https://www.python.org/dev/peps/pep-0008/

26. Rushby, J.: Quality measures and assurance for AI (artificial intelligence) software. Technical report (1988)

27. Russell, S.J., Norvig, P.: Artificial Intelligence - A Modern Approach: The Intelligent Agent Book. Prentice Hall Series in Artificial Intelligence. Prentice Hall, Upper Saddle River (1995)
28. Sculley, D., et al.: Hidden technical debt in machine learning systems. In: Advances in Neural Information Processing Systems, pp. 2503–2511 (2015)
29. Wang, J., Li, L., Zeller, A.: Better code, better sharing: on the need of analyzing Jupyter notebooks (2019)
30. Zhang, J.M., Harman, M., Ma, L., Liu, Y.: Machine learning testing: survey, landscapes and horizons. IEEE Trans. Softw. Eng. **PP**, 1 (2020)
31. Ören, T.I.: Quality assurance paradigms for artificial intelligence in modelling and simulation. Simulation **48**(4), 149–151 (1987)

Hidden Feedback Loops in Machine Learning Systems: A Simulation Model and Preliminary Results

Anton Khritankov[✉]

Moscow Institute of Physics and Technology, Dolgoprudny,
Moscow Region, Russian Federation
anton.khritankov@acm.org

Abstract. In this concept paper, we explore some of the aspects of quality of continuous learning artificial intelligence systems as they interact with and influence their environment. We study an important problem of implicit feedback loops that occurs in recommendation systems, web bulletins and price estimation systems. We demonstrate how feedback loops intervene with user behavior on an exemplary housing prices prediction system. Based on a preliminary model, we highlight sufficient existence conditions when such feedback loops arise and discuss possible solution approaches.

Keywords: Machine Learning · Continuous machine learning ·
Software quality · Feedback loop

1 Introduction

Definition of quality and requirements specification are important practices in information systems development. While in software engineering there are established quality standards like ISO 25000 series [21], machine learning (ML) engineering lacks any comparable documents. Machine learning system quality definition and evaluation is a new and active area of research.

In this paper, we consider closed loop machine learning systems - that is information systems, which behavior depends on statistical models, parameters of which are inferred from the data influenced by the system itself. These are, for example, an e-commerce web site with product recommendations, a digital library with embedded search, job postings and other digital bulletins with content search or recommendation capabilities. In contrast, web-scale search engines are not typically considered closed loop (see also [17]) because their response depends on the data out of direct control of the system, unless search personalization is employed. Non-closed loop systems also include any systems that do not use data they produce for changing their behavior, like weather forecasting systems.

The problem we study is somewhat related to the concept drift phenomenon [13]. The concept drift is an observable change in the distribution of input data

© Springer Nature Switzerland AG 2021
D. Winkler et al. (Eds.): SWQD 2021, LNBIP 404, pp. 54–65, 2021.
https://doi.org/10.1007/978-3-030-65854-0_5

that occurs over time. For closed loop systems such drift may occur as a result of changes in the user behavior due to social and cultural reasons, or because of user interaction with the system. The latter effect is called a **feedback loop**.

The difference is that concept drift usually assumes that data distribution is stationary, changes are unexpected and shall be detected and taken into account. While if a feedback loops exist, then the distribution of input data changes as a result of using the system, therefore changes are expected.

There are reasons why discovering these feedback loops is important. First, the effect of a feedback loop is not immediate and may not exhibit itself during system testing. Second, in case of continuous and lifelong machine learning systems their algorithms are able to learn from the data with little or no supervision from developers. Changes learnt from the data often constitute themselves in internal parameters and may not be directly observable nor interpretable even if shown to developers. The latter - non-observability - distinguishes feedback loops in machine learning systems from similar loops, for example, in the ordinary software-only or technical systems. What is visible and observable about feedback loops are their effects on user behavior.

Main contributions of this paper are as follows. First, we provide a simple model of a continuous machine learning system with a positive feedback loop, which is easier to study than real-world systems. Second, we propose a simulation experiment that reflects the evolution of the system being modeled. Third, based on the results from the simulation we propose a technique to detect feedback loops in industry systems and provide directions for further research.

The rest of the paper is organized as follows. In the next section we provide more background on the problem of feedback loops in machine learning systems and connect our study with related research. In Sect. 3 we demonstrate a feedback loop effect in an experiment with a housing pricing estimation system. In Sect. 4 we discuss conditions when such feedback loops may occur and how they can be discovered. Section 5 provides possible future research directions.

2   Background and Related Work

Machine Learning (ML) is an area of research in artificial intelligence (AI) that studies complex statistical models and algorithms that infer parameters of these models from the data. This process is called model training. Usually, the parameters of the model are tuned in such a way to best reflect the underlying data.

A machine learning system relies on these models with tuned parameters to provide useful functionality, for example, to make predictions or take appropriate actions. This implies that quality of such systems highly depends on the data used to train the model.

If the data is known and fixed in any given time, then it is called offline machine learning, and the available data is called a dataset. Datasets are usually split into training, development (or validation) and testing (or evaluation) parts. Training and development parts are used to infer model and training algorithm parameters correspondingly. In some cases, training and development parts may be chosen dynamically at training time, while the testing part is usually held out and is only used to evaluate the quality of the resulting model.

If the data is not fixed and comes as a stream, then it is called online or continuous machine learning. In this case, separation of incoming data is still possible but training, development and testing parts may need to be updated continuously with new data.

In supervised machine learning, the data contains expected or correct values that the model should learn to predict. In this case the quality of the model can be derived by comparing predictions with the expected values, for example, as the number of errors or empirical loss.

Prediction error can be decomposed into variance and bias. Suppose we train our model many times using different randomly chosen parts (or samples) in training and development data. A low variance model is the model that provides approximately the same predictions when trained on different parts of data, and low bias model means is the model which predictions are close to the correct values.

In the unsupervised case, the data does not contain the answers, therefore the quality is measured using relations between the model parameters or between parameters and predictions themselves.

In recent years, machine learning systems have become wide-spread and most of computer users interact with several of them every day. There is a recent survey on common problems and challenges to be solved when deploying models into production. Wan et al. [22] provide a survey on how software engineering practices differ for ML versus non-ML systems and between ML libraries and ML applications. They discover differences in requirements elicitation and software development processes that originate from uncertainty inherent to machine learning and from its dependency on available data.

Experience with developing machine learning systems in a large software company is reported in [1], emphasising 1) data management 2) model customization and reuse 3) unpredictable and non-monotonic error behavior of AI components. A recent review in [24] discusses challenges with quality and testing of machine learning systems and highlights research trends. Authors suggest more research is needed in testing for machine learning systems including testing of more tasks and algorithms, adding benchmarks and new approaches to testing.

In [3] authors describe seven projects that demonstrate challenges associated with the software engineering for machine learning systems. They identify twelve main challenges in experiment management, testing and debugging, monitoring and dependency management, privacy and ethical issues. They also include unintended feedback loops as one of the production challenges.

Another paper on challenges in machine learning systems development connects the challenges with a hidden technical debt [19]. Among other challenges, authors signify that hidden feedback loops shall be identified and removed whenever possible. Monitoring and restricting system actions are also recommended to limit the impact.

A recent review of case studies in [14] explore the development of machine learning systems from six different companies. Authors identify main challenges and map them to a taxonomy they propose that shows evaluation of how ML components are used in software-intensive system in industrial settings. Following [19] they indicate hidden feedback loops as one of the challenges when deploying models.

Positive and negative feedback loops have been also considered as a mechanism used in design of self-adaptive systems [5]. The paper signifies that studying feedback loops is important for understanding self-adaptive systems and identifies challenges that need be addressed.

In [4] authors study effects of feedback loops in complex interactions between users and advertisers during an ads auction in an online advertising system. They notice that temporarily popular ads may get permanent dominance because of positive feedback loops. Another paper [2] considers feedback loops in a context of AI systems safety, signifying instabilities and undesired side-effects associated with uncontrolled feedback loops.

In social sciences and online communication, echo chambers and filter bubbles are a similar effect produced by feedback loops in content recommendation and search systems [7,8,17]. Ensign et al. [9] describe a positive feedback loop effect in a predictive policing. Authors consider how the predictive policy system that assigns police patrols influences the city crimes data that is collected back and affects the system itself.

Results of the fairness in machine learning workshop [6] show that uncontrolled hidden feedback loops lead to decision bias. They confirm concerns put forward by [9] that if not taken into account, feedback loops effects in sociotechnical systems may result in undesired behavior affecting social communities. Authors also identify that studying dynamic and evolutionary behavior of software systems is a frontier research area.

A study of feedback loops in recommendation systems [20] suggests that for a specific class of algorithms, namely collaboration filtering, it could be possible to compensate for feedback loop effects and obtain intrinsic user preferences that are not affected by their interaction with the recommendation system.

3 Problem Statement

3.1 Motivating Example

Let us consider a website with a rental prices calculator[1]. When in use, such website would provide users with estimates of a housing or rental prices given features of the property. Some of the features may be obtained from publicly available sources and depend on house location, while others are specific to the property itself. As both buyers and sellers see the same estimate, they would consider the price as unbiased and treat it as a sort of market average price.

---

[1] Such as openrent.co.uk or zillow.com or any other similar website.

We argue that if users of such system adhere to the provided prices and choose to rent or buy a property based on the predicted price, there can be a positive feedback loop that significantly affects system and user behavior. Indeed, the possibility of the effect in an estate price prediction system (EST) was indicated in [3].

3.2   Formal Statement

As studying real world data is out of scope of this paper and may come with unrelated difficulties, let us instead consider an exemplary problem that reflects main features of the real world situation. For this purpose, we chose a well-known housing prices prediction problem on the Boston dataset [11]. Partly, because it is well-known and publicly available, and our results could be easily verified.

In order to demonstrate the feedback loop effect in a machine learning system we replicate a real-life problem in a simulation experiment.

The formal statement is as follows. We define a supervised learning regression problem [16]. Given features x_i of house i we need to predict its price $y' = f(x_i; \theta)$ so that empirical loss on a given dataset (X, y), where $X = \{x_1, ..x_n\}, y = \{y_1, ..y_n\}$, is minimized with regards to θ, that is

$$L(y, f(X; \theta)) \rightarrow \min_{\theta}. \tag{1}$$

4   Methods

4.1   Simulation Experiment

The simulation experiment is going to replicate the evolution of a real system over a period of time[2]. We aim for as simple experiment as possible to highlight the nature of the feedback loop effect and reduce the design choices.

There design choices are as follows.

– **Solution to the regression problem.** We study two different families of ML models to solve the regression problem (1): linear models and non-linear models based on ensembles of decision-trees. The choice of these is first, because of their different properties in variance and bias, and second, because they are widely applied in machine learning systems.
– **Model of user behavior.** Motivated by the housing prices problem in which users take decisions occasionally and may not return for a long time, we assume that users behave independently of each other at random and distribution of their decisions is conditioned [16] only on the predicted price and does not change over time. In a real system, users may abandon the system or stop following suggested prices thus violating the assumption.

---

[2] The source code for the experiment is available at https://github.com/prog-autom/hidden-demo.

– **Evolution of the system.** We assume that the model is retrained on schedule using the dataset that includes all user pricing decisions, whether a user followed the prediction or not.
– **Quality definition.** Quality of the predictions is measured with a widely used metric that reflects similarity of predictions with provided correct values.

Another approach could be to perform a statistical study instead of simulation. In this case, rigorous modeling of data would be required, which could be complicated considering complex data and model dependencies.

A theoretical discussion of the effect is covered in Sect. 5, where we apply theory of contractive mappings and define sufficient existence criteria for feedback loops.

4.2   Experiment Setup

The linear model $y' = X\theta + b$ is solved as Ridge regression with mean squared error loss function $L(y, y')$. The non-linear model is a stochastic gradient boosted decision tree for regression (GBR) algorithm (both as of scikit-learn implementation [18]) with Huber loss function and mean absolute error (MAE) splitting criterion, which have shown better quality and stability compared to more common squared loss function and mean-squared error (MSE) splitting criterion on this dataset.

Following a recommended practice, we perform cross-validation for hyperparameter tuning for Ridge regression and evaluate both models on held-out data. We use coefficient of determination R^2 as a measure of the model quality.

We use a simple heuristic that helps improve quality of predictions of the models. Notice that price y distribution in the dataset is not symmetric, that is, there can usually be no negative prices, $y \geq 0$. It is known from other domains that relative variation in the price is seen by consumers as more important than absolute change. That is, it is more common to see "market grew 1.5% yesterday", than "market grew 100 points". Therefore, we transform $y \leftarrow \log y$.

For the linear model we also transform the source data to zero mean and unit variance before training, which is the recommended practice.

In order to simulate different levels of closedness of the system, we assume that a user either ignores the predicted price with probability $1 - p$, either uses the prediction with p. If uses the prediction, a user chooses a logarithm of the price $\log z_i$ (recall the transform) randomly by sampling it from the Normal distribution $N(f(x_i; \theta), s\sigma_f^2)$, where σ_f^2 is the model's mean squared error on held-out data and $s > 0$ is an experiment parameter that indicates adherence.

Because of logarithmic scaling of target variable y, in order to get actual prices, we need to exponentiate the predicted values.

The experiment starts with 30% of original data at round $r = 1$. The first model is trained with cross-validation on the 80% part of the starting data giving $\theta^{[r=1]}$ and evaluated on the rest held-out 20% of the data. Then on each step $t \geq 0$ a user takes a prediction $y'_k = f(x_k; \theta^{[r]})$, $k = 0.3n + t$ from the model and decides on the price z_k as specified above.

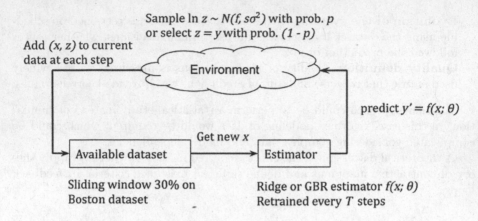

Fig. 1. Feedback loop experiment setup

The actual price z_k that a user has decided upon and features x_k are appended to the current data and the first item is removed so overall size of current data remains constant. This is equivalent to using a sliding window of the most recent 30% of data with some of original prices y_k in the dataset replaced with user decisions z_k.

After each T steps the round increments $r \leftarrow r + 1$ and the model is retrained with cross-validation on current data, which is again split on training 80% and held-out 20% parts giving $\theta^{[r]}$.

The procedure repeats while there are unseen points available $0.3n + t \leq n$. Thus, at each round we know the coefficient of determination $R^2(r)$ for both models.

4.3   Results and Observations

We repeated the experiment several times for specific parameter values and provide the aggregated results below.

The representative results are shown at Fig. 2 and Fig. 3. In both cases the model starts getting higher $R^2(r)$ score on held-out data as the number of rounds increases, and tends to $R^2 = 1.0$. Despite the linear regression model having lower quality score in the beginning, it starts outperforming the gradient boosting tree regression (GBR) algorithm after several rounds.

If all users adhere to predictions of the system, that is, the usage parameter p gets closer to 1.0, the sequence $R^2(r)$ tends to 1.0 faster. When adherence $p < 0.5$ the R^2 may not get to 1.0 and even decrease as a result of users random sampling of z_k, which are added to the current data.

When adherence parameter s is close to 0.0 and the model has high initial R^2 the sequence proceeds faster to 1.0. Large values of $s > 0.5$ may lead to a lot of noise being added to current data over rounds. Experimentally, $s < 1.25$ at $p = 0.75$ is needed for $R^2(r)$ to converge close to 1.0 with the linear model, and $s < 0.5$ with the GBR algorithm.

When the number of steps between rounds T gets closer to 1.0 the $R^2(r)$ of the GBR algorithm fluctuates and does not grow to 1.0. Contrary to the linear model, for which $R^2(r)$ tends to 1.0 for a much wider range of parameters.

For reference, in a completely closed loop system, we would have $p = 1.0$ and $p = 0.0$ for a completely open loop system.

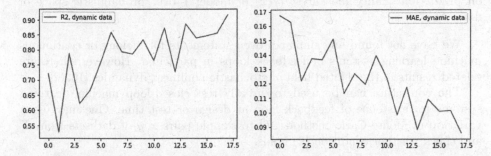

Fig. 2. Positive feedback loop on prediction quality. Model: GBR, steps before retraining $T = 20$, usage $p = 0.75$ and adherence $s = 0.2$

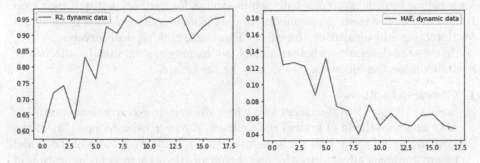

Fig. 3. Positive feedback loop on prediction quality. Model: Ridge, steps before retraining $T = 20$, usage $p = 0.75$ and adherence $s = 0.2$

5   Analysis and Discussion

5.1   Existence Conditions for a Positive Feedback Loop

It looks like that convergence of the $R^2(r)$ or other quality metrics when round $r \to \infty$ requires that the deviation of the observed data from model predictions should decrease as the number of rounds grows. If it is so, then the deviation would converge to zero and the corresponding model would provide for the minimum possible error with probability equals to one.

Let us consider a probabilistic space of datasets X. A closed-loop system can the be represented as a mapping T that transforms any dataset $x \in X$ to another dataset $x' \in X$. That is a mapping $T : X \to X$ defines a single user interaction with the system. Then we can draft the following.

Conjecture 1 (sufficient condition for existence of a positive feedback loop). A positive feedback loop in a system $T : X \to X$ exists if

$$\forall x, y \in X : d(R_f(T(x)), R_f(T(y))) \leq A \cdot d(R_f(x), R_f(y)), a.s. \qquad (2)$$

where $0 < A < 1$ is a constant, and $d(r_1, r_2)$ is a distance metric defined on prediction quality measures $R_f(x)$ of model f over probabilistic space of datasets X.

We have not found any similar proven statements for lifelong or continuous machine learning systems or feedback loops in particular. However, there are related results in the related field of stochastic nonlinear dynamics [10,12].

The conjecture can be used to directly test closed-loop machine learning systems for existence of feedback loop at design or test time. One may use a variation of Monte-Carlo method [16] to sample pairs x, y of datasets from X and check whether condition (2) holds.

5.2   Checklist for Detecting Feedback Loops

Following from our findings, we suggest that requirements analysis and review for machine learning systems shall include studies for feedback loops. If such loop is possible, then system requirements should include implementation of measures for detecting and measuring the effect. Therefore, making it observable.

In order to determine whether a machine learning system may be affected by feedback loops the following checks may be performed:

1. **Check data flows**
   Look at the problem statement and where the system receives data from. One may apply methods of system dynamics to discover causal loops [15]. If the system receives data from the same users that rely on predictions of the model or environment affected by the user behavior, then there is an indication of possible feedback loop.
2. **Check usage scenarios**
   Check the expected impact of the system on user behavior and the data received from users and the environment. If usage p and adherence s parameters may get $p > 0.5$ and $s < 1.0$ then there is a possibility of feedback loop.
3. **Check sufficient conditions for feedback loop**
   Given an indication of a possible feedback loop, we can use Conjecture 1 to check for existence of feedback loops at system *test time* using a Monte-Carlo method. For the experiment, select a baseline model and training algorithm, preferably with low variance. Then sample a series of dataset pairs from the environment as described in the previous section. If conditions (2) hold then there will be a feedback loop when the system is implemented and deployed.

Another option is to check for feedback loops at *run-time*. Consider selecting a baseline model, which parameters are learnt from the data once and remain fixed. According to the *No Free Lunch* theorem [23], the quality of predictions of the baseline model shall not improve over time. And if it does improve, this indicates a presence of a positive feedback loop.

In addition, a range of concept drift detection methods may be used [13].

6   Future Research

Solution to the problem of detection of hidden feedback loops would contribute to more reliable and fair decisions made by machine learning systems [6].

Future research may include formal proof of Conjecture 1 on the existence of feedback loops. Suggestions given in this paper will need to be confirmed empirically on real-life closed loop systems.

As a recent survey shows [24] a study of feedback loops is not usually performed during machine learning system design and quality evaluation. We propose to include observability of feedback loops in the quality criteria for machine learning systems.

Additional guidelines on satisfying the quality criteria and checking feedback loop existence conditions should be developed as well as supporting software tools.

It should be investigated further, what properties of the model or algorithms lead to feedback loops. For example, if we have a 100% accurate algorithm, it can be shown not to produce the feedback loop. Some variance and bias are needed for a model to be able to influence the data.

Despite being reported in several real-world systems [2–4,7–9,17] more empirical studies are needed that further specify conditions for existence of feedback loops and test whether proposed detection techniques are effective.

7   Conclusion

Machine learning systems constitute a growing part on the software systems landscape. Being able to continuously learn models from available data without participation or supervision of engineers and researchers such systems are susceptible to hidden feedback loops.

In this paper we studied a feedback loop problem in closed loop continuous learning systems. We demonstrated and quantified the effect on an exemplary housing prices recommendation system. Based on preliminary findings and analysis of the experiment results, we propose specific measures to check for and detect feedback loops in machine learning systems.

Further research could be directed towards practical evaluation of the proposed design and test-time checklist for existence of feedback loops and determining properties of algorithms that make them susceptible to feedback loops.

Acknowledgments. Authors are thankful to the anonymous reviewers whose useful feedback helped to improve the paper.

References

1. Amershi, S., et al.: Software engineering for machine learning: a case study. In: Proceedings of the IEEE/ACM 41st International Conference on Software Engineering: Software Engineering in Practice (ICSE-SEIP 2019), pp. 291–300. IEEE (2019)
2. Amodei, D., Olah, C., Steinhardt, J., Christiano, P., Schulman, J., Mané, D.: Concrete problems in AI safety. arXiv preprint arXiv:1606.06565 (2016)
3. Arpteg, A., Brinne, B., Crnkovic-Friis, L., Bosch, J.: Software engineering challenges of deep learning. In: Proceedings of the 44th Euromicro Conference on Software Engineering and Advanced Applications (SEAA 2018), pp. 50–59. IEEE (2018)
4. Bottou, L., et al.: Counterfactual reasoning and learning systems: the example of computational advertising. J. Mach. Learn. Res. **14**(1), 3207–3260 (2013)
5. Brun, Y., et al.: Engineering self-adaptive systems through feedback loops. In: Cheng, B.H.C., de Lemos, R., Giese, H., Inverardi, P., Magee, J. (eds.) Software Engineering for Self-Adaptive Systems. LNCS, vol. 5525, pp. 48–70. Springer, Heidelberg (2009). https://doi.org/10.1007/978-3-642-02161-9_3
6. Chouldechova, A., Roth, A.: The frontiers of fairness in machine learning. arXiv preprint arXiv:1810.08810 (2018)
7. Colleoni, E., Rozza, A., Arvidsson, A.: Echo chamber or public sphere? predicting political orientation and measuring political homophily in twitter using big data. J. Commun. **64**(2), 317–332 (2014)
8. DiFranzo, D., Gloria-Garcia, K.: Filter bubbles and fake news. XRDS Crossroads ACM Mag. Students **23**(3), 32–35 (2017)
9. Ensign, D., Friedler, S.A., Neville, S., Scheidegger, C., Venkatasubramanian, S.: Runaway feedback loops in predictive policing (2017)
10. Hadzic, O., Pap, E.: Fixed Point Theory in Probabilistic Metric Spaces, vol. 536. Springer Science & Business Media, Dordrecht (2013)
11. Harrison Jr., D., Rubinfeld, D.L.: Hedonic housing prices and the demand for clean air. J. Environ. Econ. Manage. **5**, 81–102 (1978)
12. Joshi, M.C., Bose, R.K.: Some Topics in Nonlinear Functional Analysis. John Wiley & Sons, New York (1985)
13. Lu, J., Liu, A., Dong, F., Gu, F., Gama, J., Zhang, G.: Learning under concept drift: a review. IEEE Trans. Knowl. Data Eng. **31**(12), 2346–2363 (2018)
14. Lwakatare, L.E., Raj, A., Bosch, J., Olsson, H.H., Crnkovic, I.: A taxonomy of software engineering challenges for machine learning systems: an empirical investigation. In: Kruchten, P., Fraser, S., Coallier, F. (eds.) XP 2019. LNBIP, vol. 355, pp. 227–243. Springer, Cham (2019). https://doi.org/10.1007/978-3-030-19034-7_14
15. Martin Jr, D., Prabhakaran, V., Kuhlberg, J., Smart, A., Isaac, W.S.: Participatory problem formulation for fairer machine learning through community based system dynamics. arXiv preprint arXiv:2005.07572 (2020)
16. Murphy, K.P.: Machine Learning: A Probabilistic Perspective. MIT Press, Cambridge (2012)
17. Pariser, E.: The Filter Bubble: What the Internet is Hiding from You. Penguin, New York (2011)
18. Pedregosa, F., et al.: Scikit-learn: Machine learning in python. J. Mach. Learn. Res. **12**, 2825–2830 (2011)
19. Sculley, D., et al.: Hidden technical debt in machine learning systems. In: Advances in Neural Information Processing Systems, pp. 2503–2511 (2015)

20. Sinha, A., Gleich, D.F., Ramani, K.: Deconvolving feedback loops in recommender systems. In: Advances in Neural Information Processing Systems, pp. 3243–3251 (2016)
21. Suryn, W., Abran, A., April, A.: ISO/IEC SQuaRE: the second generation of standards for software product quality (2003)
22. Wan, Z., Xia, X., Lo, D., Murphy, G.C.: How does machine learning change software development practices? IEEE Trans. Softw. Eng. **9**, 4492–4500 (2019)
23. Wolpert, D.H., Macready, W.G.: No free lunch theorems for optimization. IEEE Trans. Evol. Comput. **1**(1), 67–82 (1997)
24. Zhang, J.M., Harman, M., Ma, L., Liu, Y.: Machine learning testing: survey, landscapes and horizons. IEEE Trans. Softw. Eng. (2020). https://doi.org/10.1109/TSE.2019.2962027

The AIQ Meta-Testbed: Pragmatically Bridging Academic AI Testing and Industrial Q Needs

Markus Borg[1,2(✉)]

[1] RISE Research Institutes of Sweden AB, Lund, Sweden
markus.borg@ri.se
[2] Department of Computer Science, Lund University, Lund, Sweden

Abstract. AI solutions seem to appear in any and all application domains. As AI becomes more pervasive, the importance of quality assurance increases. Unfortunately, there is no consensus on what artificial intelligence means and interpretations range from simple statistical analysis to sentient humanoid robots. On top of that, quality is a notoriously hard concept to pinpoint. What does this mean for AI quality? In this paper, we share our working definition and a pragmatic approach to address the corresponding quality assurance with a focus on testing. Finally, we present our ongoing work on establishing the AIQ Meta-Testbed.

Keywords: Artificial intelligence · Machine learning · Quality assurance · Software testing · Testbed

1 Introduction

The number of AI applications is constantly growing. Across diverse domains, enterprises want to harness AI technology to explore the lucrative promises expressed by AI advocates. As AI becomes pervasive, there is inevitably a need to build trust in this type of software. Furthermore, critical AI is on the rise, i.e., applications will not be restricted to entertainment and games. AI is already fundamental in many business-critical applications such as ad optimization and recommendation systems. As the technology further evolves, many believe that safety-critical AI will soon become commonplace in the automotive [1] and medical domains [2]. Other examples of critical AI, with other types of quality requirements, will be found in the finance industry and the public sector. Unfortunately, how to best approach Quality Assurance (QA) for AI applications remains an open question.

A fundamental issue originates already in the terminology, i.e., the concept of "AI quality". First, there are several different definitions of AI, and their interpretations range from simple statistical analysis to the sentient humanoid robotics of the science fiction literature. Furthermore, AI appears to be a moving target, as what was considered AI when the term was coined in the 1950s would

D. Winkler et al. (Eds.): SWQD 2021, LNBIP 404, pp. 66–77, 2021.
https://doi.org/10.1007/978-3-030-65854-0_6

hardly qualify as AI today. Second, in the same vein, quality is a notoriously difficult aspect to pinpoint [3]. Quality is a multi-dimensional patchwork of different product aspects that influences the user's experience. Moreover, quality is highly subjective and largely lies in the eye of the beholder. Taken together, AI quality is a truly challenging concept to approach, i.e., a subjective mishmash of user experience regarding a type of technology with unclear boundaries that also change over time. There is a need for pragmatic interpretations to help advance research and practice related to AI quality – we provide ours in Sect. 3.

Contemporary AI solutions are dominated by Machine Learning (ML) and in particular supervised learning. A pragmatic first step would be to initially focus QA accordingly. As development of systems that rely on supervised learning introduces new challenges, QA must inevitably adapt. No longer is all logic expressed by programmers in source code instructions, instead ML models are trained on large sets of annotated data. Andrej Karpathy, AI Director at Tesla, refers to this paradigm of solution development as "Software 2.0" and claims that for many applications that require a mapping from input to output, it is easier to collect and annotate appropriate data than to explicitly write the mapping function.[1] As we embark on the AI quality journey, we argue that methods for QA of "Software 2.0" should evolve first – we refer to this as *MLware*.

The rest of this paper is organized as follows. Section 2 motivates the importance of MLware QA, elaborates on the intrinsic challenges, and presents closely related work. Section 3 introduces the working definitions used in our work on establishing the AIQ Meta-Testbed, which is further described in Sect. 4. Finally, Sect. 5 concludes our position paper.

2 Background and Related Work

Fueled by Internet-scale data and enabled by massive compute, ML using Deep Neural Networks (DNN), i.e., neural networks with several layers, has revolutionized several application areas. Success stories include computer vision, speech recognition, and machine translation. We will focus the discussion on DNNs, but many of the involved QA issues apply also to other families of ML, e.g., support vector machines, logistic regression, and random forests – software that is not only coded, but also trained.

From a QA perspective, developing systems based on DNNs constitutes a paradigm shift compared to conventional systems [4]. No longer do human engineers explicitly express all logic in source code, instead DNNs are trained using enormous amounts of historical data. A state-of-the-art DNN might be composed of hundreds of millions of parameter weights that is neither applicable for code review nor code coverage testing [5] – best practices in industry and also mandated by contemporary safety standards. As long as ML applications are restricted to non-critical entertainment applications (e.g., video games and smartphone camera effects) this might not be an issue. However, when ML applications are integrated into critical systems, they must be trustworthy.

---

[1] bit.ly/3dKeUEH.

The automotive domain is currently spearheading work on dependable ML, reflected by work on the emerging safety standard ISO/PAS 21448. DNNs are key enablers for vehicle environmental perception, which is a prerequisite for autonomous features such as lane departure detection, path planning, and vehicle tracking. While DNNs have been reported to outperform human classification accuracy for specific tasks, they will occasionally misclassify new input. Recent work shows that DNNs trained for perception can drastically change their output if only a few pixels change [6]. The last decade resulted in many beaten ML benchmarks, but as illustrated by this example, there is a pressing need to close the gap between ML application development and its corresponding QA.

There are established approaches to QA for conventional software, i.e., software expressed in source code. Best practices have been captured in numerous textbooks over the years, e.g., by Schulmeyer [7], Galin [8], Mistrik *et al.* [9], and Walkinshaw [3]. Developers write source code that can be inspected by others as part of QA. As a complement, static code analysis tools can be used to support source code quality. Unfortunately, the logic encapsulated in a trained ML model cannot be targeted by QA approaches that work on the source code level. ML models in general, and DNN models in particular, are treated as black boxes. While there is growing interest in research on explainable AI [10], interpreting the inner workings of ML is still an open problem. This is a substantial issue when explainability is fundamental, e.g., when safety certification is required [11] or when demonstrating legal compliance [12] (such as GDPR or absence of illegal discrimination in the trained model).

On the other hand, source code inspection and analysis are also not sufficient tools to perform QA of conventional software systems. During development, software solutions rapidly grow into highly complex systems whose QA rarely can be restricted to analysis – although substantial research effort has been dedicated to formal methods [13] including formal verification in model-driven engineering [14]. In practice, software QA revolves around well-defined processes [15,16] and a backbone of software testing. Software testing, i.e., learning about the system by executing it, is the quintessential approach to software QA [17–19].

In the software engineering community, there is momentum on evolving practices to replace ad-hoc development of AI-enabled systems by systematic engineering approaches. A textbook by Hulten on "Building Intelligent Systems" [20] is recommended reading in related courses by Kästner at Carnegie Mellon University [21] and Jamshidi at University of South Carolina. Kästner also provides an annotated bibliography of related academic research[2], as does the SE4ML group at Leiden Institute of Advanced Computer Science[3], recently summarized in an academic paper [22]. Bosch *et al.* recently presented a research agenda for engineering of AI systems [23], sharing what they consider the most important activities to reach production-quality AI systems.

In recent years, numerous papers proposed novel testing techniques tailored for ML. Zhang *et al.* conducted a comprehensive survey of 144 papers on ML

---

[2] https://github.com/ckaestne/seaibib.
[3] https://github.com/SE-ML/awesome-seml.

testing [24], defined as "any activities designed to reveal ML bugs" where an ML bug is "any imperfection in a machine learning item that causes a discordance between the existing and the required conditions." Riccio *et al.* conducted another secondary study, analyzing 70 primary studies on functional testing of ML-based systems [25]. The authors do not use the term "bug" for misclassifications, as any ML component will sometimes fail to generalize. We agree with this view, and avoid terms such as ML bugs, model bugs and the like when referring to functional inefficiencies of MLware.

3   AI Quality Assurance – Working Definitions

As discussed in Sect. 1, AI quality is a challenging concept to define. Consequently, QA for AI is at least as hard to specify. Still, we need a working definition to initiate efforts in this direction. In this section, we present the rationale behind our working definition of AI quality and AI quality assurance. Moreover, we introduce several related terms we use in collaborations with industry partners.

The original definition of AI from the 1950s is *"the science and engineering of making intelligent machines"*. Unfortunately, this definition turns AI into a moving target, as expectations on what constitutes an intelligent machine change over time – a computer program for logistics optimization in a warehouse would have been considered intelligent in the 1950s whereas it now could be part of an undergraduate computer science course. Since the term AI was introduced, it has often been used to refer to software solutions of the future, displaying increasingly human-like capabilities. The notation of "intelligence" is still common when referring to the gist of AI/ML applications, as in Hulten's textbook [20], but ideally we want a definition that remains the same over time.

We argue that the most useful view on AI is to consider it as the next wave of automation in the digital society. Extrapolating from the sequence 1) digitization, 2) digitalization, and 3) digital transformation [26], we consider AI as the next enabling wave in the same direction – allowing automation of more complex tasks than before. Our working definition of AI is *"software that enables automation of tasks that normally would require human intelligence"*. While still imprecise, the definition is good enough for us to later define a delimited subset of AI that deserves our research focus.

Consulting the well-known textbook on AI by Russell and Norvig is one approach to explore the scope of AI [27]. The table of contents lists concepts such as searching, game playing, logic, planning, probabilistic reasoning, natural language processing, perception, robotics, and, of course, learning – all important components when mimicking human intelligence. The textbook clearly shows that AI is more than ML. On the other hand, we argue that conventional software QA and testing can be applied to all AI techniques that are implemented in source code. Supervised and unsupervised learning, however, involves a transfer of control from source code to data. Research efforts on QA tailored for this new paradigm are what now would provide the highest return-on-investment. We need to focus on ML-enabled software – we refer to this as *MLware* for short.

Figure 1 illustrates our view on MLware. The future of systems engineering will combine hardware and software components, but the software part needs to be differentiated. A subset of software represents the fuzzy area of AI. We accept that this subset is neither clear-cut nor consistent over time. MLware is a subset of AI that rely on supervised and/or unsupervised learning. All MLware is not made the same. From a QA perspective, we need to distinguish between *trained MLware* that does not learn post deployment and *learning MLware* that keeps improving as new experience is collected post deployment. Learning MLware can be further divided into offline learning (triggered re-training in batches) and online learning (continuous update of trained models).

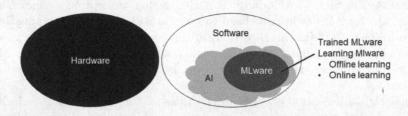

Fig. 1. MLware in context.

One might wonder where Reinforcement Learning (RL) fits in our working definition of MLware. Currently, we exclude RL from MLware. The rationale is that in RL, the exploration and exploitation of the learning agent is implemented in source code. RL shares characteristics of both searching and automatic control. We posit that software testing approaches proposed for self-adaptive systems could be generalized to RL [28,29], and thus the best use of research resources is to focus on supervised and unsupervised learning – the dominating types of ML in practical applications.

A well-cited experience report by Sculley and his Google colleagues presents the vast and complex infrastructure required for successful MLware [30]. The authors describe this in terms of hidden technical debt of ML (cf. the lower part of Fig. 2). Building on this discussion, and the expression that "data is the new oil", our view is that data indeed fuels ML, but conventional source code is still in the driving seat, i.e., MLware is fueled by data and driven by code (cf. the upper part of Fig. 2). From this standpoint, it is obvious that conventional approaches to software QA remain essential in the new data-intensive paradigm of MLware. Moreover, just as software QA is dominated by software testing, we expect MLware QA to be dominated by MLware testing.

The phenomenon of software quality has been addressed in plentiful publications. Among other things, this has resulted in standardized software quality models such as ISO/IEC 25010. As MLware still is software, and certainly driven by source code, the existing quality models remain foundational. The sister standard, ISO/IEC 25012 Data Quality Model, adds a complementary data dimension to the quality discussion. As MLware is fueled by data, this standard is also highly relevant. Our working definition of AI quality is largely an amalgamation of the definitions provided by these two standards in the ISO/IEC 25000 series.

As mentioned in Sect. 2, there is no consensus in how to refer to issues resulting in MLware misclassifications. Bug is not a suitable term to cover all functional insufficiencies, given its strong connotation to source code defects. Still, we need a new similarly succinct term in the context of MLware. We propose *snag* to refer to the difference between existing and required behaviors of MLware interwoven of data and source code. The root cause of a snag can be a bug either in the learning code or the infrastructure [24], but it is often related to inadequate training data – we call the latter phenomenon a *dug*.

Figure 2 presents an overview of our perspective on issues detected in MLware. In the upper left, MLware is illustrated as a type of software that interweaves data (the fuel) and source code (at the helm) to produce output. If a discordance is observed, we call for a snag in the MLware fabric. Assuming that the requirements are valid and the observer interprets them correctly, root causes of snags include bugs and dugs as well as environment issues. The lower part of the figure illustrates the technical debt in machine learning as described by Sculley *et al.* [30]. Bugs can reside in the ML code (the white box), e.g., calling deprecated API methods or incorrect use of tensor shapes [31]. On the other hand, there might also be bugs in the rest of the infrastructure. While the illustrated technical debt revolves around data, all gray boxes will also depend on source code, from small exploratory scripts to mature open source libraries – and the large systems enabling MLware operations [20].

To summarize this section, our position is that research on QA for AI would benefit from adhering to the definitions presented in Table 1.

4 AIQ – An AI Meta-Testbed

Based on the working definitions in Sect. 3, we plan to support AI QA by establishing an AI meta-testbed. A testbed is a venue that provides a controlled environment to evaluate technical concepts. Under current circumstances, in the middle of the ongoing AI boom[4], we believe that the establishment of a testbed for testing MLware testing would be the most valuable contribution to AI QA. Assessing the effectiveness of different testing techniques in a controlled setting is not a new idea [34], neither is the concept of testing test cases [35] – but a testbed dedicated to MLware testing is novel. We call it the AIQ Meta-Testbed[5].

Successful MLware development requires a close connection to the operational environment. The same need has shaped software development at Internet companies, resulting in DevOps – a combination of philosophies, practices, and tools to reduce the time between development and operations while preserving quality [36]. Key enablers are Continuous Integration and Deployment (CI/CD). DevOps that emphasize MLware development is often referred to as

---

[4] Well aware of the two previous "AI winters", periods with less interest and funding due to inflated expectations.

[5] metatest.ai.

Table 1. Working definitions of key terms related to the AIQ Meta-Testbed.

Term	Definition	Comments
AI	A subset of software that automates tasks that normally would require human intelligence	MLware, interwoven by data and source code, is the most precise term to describe our research interest. On the other hand, AI is a dominant term in industry and news media. We propose a pragmatic sacrifice of scientific preciseness in favour of industrial and societal relevance. In practice, we treat AI as synonymous with MLware in discussions with clients
MLware	A subset of AI that, fueled by data, realizes functionality through supervised and/or unsupervised learning	
MLware Testing	Any activity that aims to learn about MLware by executing it	The typical goal of testing is detecting differences between existing and required behavior [32]. Other possible testing goals include exploratory testing and compliance testing
AI Quality	The capability of MLware to satisfy stated and implied needs under specified conditions while the underlying data satisfy the requirements specific to the application and its context	MLware combines data and conventional source code, thus we propose the amalgamation of corresponding quality definitions from the IEC/ISO 25000 series. Our proposal is in line with discussions by Felderer *et al.* in the context of testing data-intensive systems [33]
AI Quality Assurance	Any systematic process to provide confidence that the desired AI Quality is maintained	QA encompasses many activities throughout the product lifecycle. However, in current AI discussions with clients, we primarily interpret it as MLware testing
Snag	Any imperfection in MLware that causes a discordance between the existing and the required conditions	There is an ongoing discussion in the research community about how to refer to MLware misclassifications [25]. We argue against using the term bug whenever there is unexpected output. Instead, we propose calling it a snag in the MLware fabric
Bug	A source code defect that causes a discordance between the existing and the required conditions	The term bug has a firmly established meaning, thus we suggest restricting its use to source code. As MLware is driven by code, bugs can cause snags
Dug	A data inadequacy that causes a discordance between the existing and the required conditions	With bugs reserved for source code defects, we need a novel expression for the data counterpart. The new term must be a worthy match for the succinct "bug". Currently, we call them "dugs"

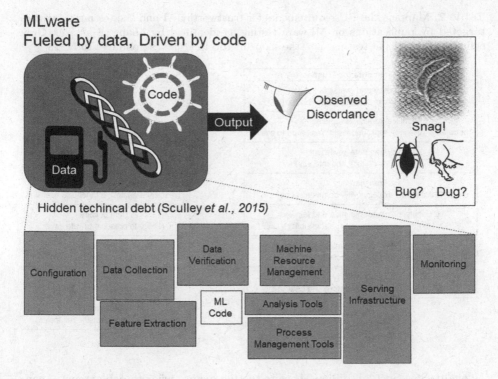

Fig. 2. MLware interwoven by data and code. Observed discordances in the output (snags) can originate in source code defects (bugs) or data inadequacies (dugs).

MLOps [37], effectively adding Continuous Training (CT) to the mix. The focus on continuousness is stressed in illustrations by the infinity symbol.

Trust is fundamental for a successful product or service embedding MLware. In 2019, an expert group set up by the European Commission published ethics guidelines for trustworthy AI[6]. As part of the guidelines, seven key requirements are introduced. Table 2 shows a mapping between the EU requirements and the testing properties identified in the survey by Zhang et al. [24]. Our preliminary analysis indicates that all but one requirement has (to some extent) been targeted by academic research. Thus, we believe the time is right for systematic meta-testing in an MLOps context.

Figure 3 presents an overview of the AIQ Meta-Testbed in the MLOps context. We will set up a contemporary MLOps pipeline to allow controlled experiments in the lab while still providing an environment relevant to industry practice. Test automation is the backbone of MLOps, and MLware testing occurs in several phases during the MLware engineering lifecycle [24] (cf. the textboxes in Fig. 3). First, the standard practice during model training is to split data into training, validation, and test subsets. We refer to this type of ML model testing

---

[6] ec.europa.eu/digital-single-market/en/news/ethics-guidelines-trustworthy-ai.

Table 2. Mapping the EU requirements for trustworthy AI and the testing properties targeted by publications on MLware testing as identified by Zhang *et al.* [24]. Gray cells show functional testing, i.e., the scope of Riccio *et al.*'s secondary study [25]

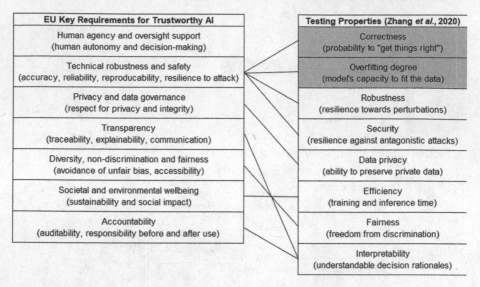

as evaluation. Second, offline MLware testing occurs prior to deployment – conducted on different testing levels (input data, ML model, integration, system) and with varying access levels of the MLware under test (white-box, data-box, black-box) as defined by Riccio *et al.* [25]. Third, online MLware testing occurs after deployment. Common examples include A/B testing and runtime monitoring to detect distributional shifts.

The AIQ Meta-Testbed will primarily focus on offline MLware testing (the solid-border textbox in Fig. 3). We plan to enable meta-testing by providing a *control panel* for toggling testing techniques (C) in Fig. 3) corresponding to the testing properties in Table 2, controlled *fault-injection* (A) (e.g., bug/dug injection, hyperparameter changes, mutation operators) and state-of-the-art *test input generation* (B) (e.g., search-based testing, GAN-based synthesis, metamorphic relations, and adequacy-driven generation). The results from both MLware testing and meta-testing will be presented in dashboards (D).

Extrapolating from the publication trends reported in the recent secondary studies [24, 25], there will be an avalanche of MLware testing papers in the next years. Staying on top of the research will become a considerable challenge and for practitioners with limited experience in reading academic papers, the challenge will be insurmountable – motivating the need to create an overview and shortlisting the most promising techniques.

Activities at the AIQ Meta-Testbed will include external replications of studies on MLware testing. By performing controlled meta-testing of the shortlisted techniques, we will be able to provide evidence-based recommendations on what

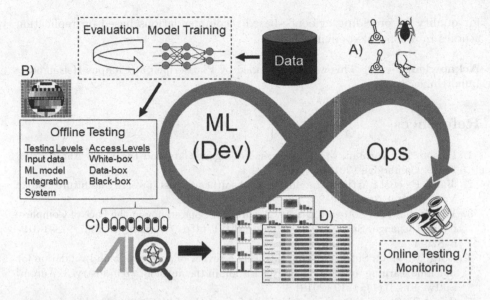

Fig. 3. The AIQ Meta-Testbed in the MLOps context. We will focus on providing A) fault-injection, B) test input generation for offline testing, C) a control panel for toggling offline testing techniques, and D) presenting the results in dashboards.

techniques to use and in which contexts. The controlled environment of the AIQ Meta-Testbed will enable exploration of applied research questions, such as:

- Which contextual factors influence the MLware test effectiveness the most?
- Which proposed MLware testing techniques scale to very large DNNs?
- How to best integrate MLware testing in an MLOps pipeline?
- What should be done to limit test maintenance in an MLware testing context?
- After observing a snag, how to support the subsequent root cause analysis?

5   Summary and Concluding Remarks

AI is becoming a pervasive subset of software, thus the elusive concepts of AI quality and QA are increasingly important. We argue that pragmatic interpretations are needed to advance the field, and introduce a working definition of MLware as a subset of software within AI that realizes functionality through machine learning by interweaving data and source code. Furthermore, we define AI quality as "the capability of MLware to satisfy stated and implied needs under specified conditions while the underlying data satisfy the requirements specific to the application and its context". We recommend that AI QA first and foremost should be interpreted as MLware testing and that the term bug shall be reserved for source code defects – instead we propose "snag" to refer to observed discordances in the MLware fabric. Finally, we present the AIQ Meta-Testbed – bridging academic research on MLware testing and industrial needs for quality by providing evidence-based recommendations based on replication studies in a controlled environment.

Acknowledgments. This work was funded by Plattformen at Campus Helsingborg, Lund University.

References

1. Lipson, H., Kurman, M.: Driverless: Intelligent Cars and the Road Ahead. MIT Press, Cambridge (2016)
2. Jiang, F., et al.: Artificial intelligence in healthcare: past, present and future. Stroke Vasc. Neurol. **2**(4), 230–243 (2017)
3. Walkinshaw, N.: Software Quality Assurance: Consistency in the Face of Complexity and Change. Springer, Heidelberg (2017). https://doi.org/10.1007/978-3-319-64822-4
4. Borg, M., et al.: Safely entering the deep: a review of verification and validation for machine learning and a challenge elicitation in the automotive industry. J. Autom. Softw. Eng. **1**(1), 1–19 (2019)
5. Salay, R., Queiroz, R., Czarnecki, K.: An Analysis of ISO 26262: Machine Learning and Safety in Automotive Software. SAE Technical Paper 2018–01-1075 (2018)
6. Azulay, A., Weiss, Y.: Why do deep convolutional networks generalize so poorly to small image transformations? J. Mach. Learn. Res. **20**, 25 (2019)
7. Schulmeyer, G.: Handbook Of Software Quality Assurance, 1st edn. Prentice Hall, Upper Saddle River (1987)
8. Galin, D.: Software Quality Assurance: From Theory to Implementation. Pearson, Harlow (2003)
9. Mistrik, I., Soley, R.M., Ali, N., Grundy, J., Tekinerdogan, B. (eds.): Software Quality Assurance: In Large Scale and Complex Software-Intensive Systems. Morgan Kaufmann, Waltham (2016)
10. Adadi, A., Berrada, M.: Peeking inside the black-box: a survey on explainable artificial intelligence (XAI). IEEE Access **6**, 52138–52160 (2018)
11. Borg, M.: Explainability first! Cousteauing the depths of neural networks to argue safety. In: Greenyer, J., Lochau, M., Vogel, T., (eds.) Explainable Software for Cyber-Physical Systems (ES4CPS): Report from the GI Dagstuhl Seminar 19023, pp. 26–27 (2019)
12. Vogelsang, A., Borg, M.: Requirements engineering for machine learning: perspectives from data scientists. In: Proceedings of the 27th International Requirements Engineering Conference Workshops, pp. 245–251 (2019)
13. Weyns, D., et al.: A survey of formal methods in self-adaptive systems. In: Proceedings of the 5th International Conference on Computer Science and Software Engineering, pp. 67–79 (2012)
14. Gonzalez, C.A., Cabot, J.: Formal verification of static software models in MDE: a systematic review. Inf. Softw. Tech. **56**(8), 821–838 (2014)
15. Herbsleb, J., et al.: Software quality and the capability maturity model. Commun. ACM **40**(6), 30–40 (1997)
16. Ashrafi, N.: The impact of software process improvement on quality: theory and practice. Inf. Manag. **40**(7), 677–690 (2003)
17. Gelperin, D., Hetzel, B.: The growth of software testing. Commun. ACM **31**(6), 687–695 (1988)

18. Orso, A., Rothermel, G.: Software testing: a research travelogue (2000–2014). In: Future of Software Engineering Proceedings, pp. 117–132 (2014)
19. Kassab, M., DeFranco, J.F., Laplante, P.A.: Software testing: the state of the practice. IEEE Softw. **34**(5), 46–52 (2017)
20. Hulten, G.: Building Intelligent Systems: A Guide to Machine Learning Engineering, 1st edn. Apress, New York (2018)
21. Kästner, C., Kang, E.: Teaching Software Engineering for AI-Enabled Systems. arXiv:2001.06691 [cs], January 2020
22. Serban, A., van der Blom, K., Hoos, H., Visser, J.: Adoption and effects of software engineering best practices in machine learning. In: Proceedings of the 14th International Symposium on Empirical Software Engineering and Measurement (2020)
23. Bosch, J., Crnkovic, I., Olsson, H.H.: Engineering AI Systems: A Research Agenda. arXiv:2001.07522 [cs], January 2020
24. Zhang, J.M., et al.: Machine learning testing: survey, landscapes and horizons. IEEE Trans. Softw. Eng. (2020). (Early Access)
25. Vincenzo, R., Jahangirova, G., Stocco, A., Humbatova, N., Weiss, M., Tonella, P.: Testing machine learning based systems: a systematic mapping. Empirical Softw. Eng. **25**, 5193–5254 (2020)
26. Schallmo, D.R.A., Williams, C.A.: History of digital transformation. Digital Transformation Now!. SB, pp. 3–8. Springer, Cham (2018). https://doi.org/10.1007/978-3-319-72844-5_2
27. Russell, S., Norvig, P.: Artificial Intelligence: A Modern Approach, 3rd edn. Pearson, Upper Saddle River (2009)
28. Cai, K.Y.: Optimal software testing and adaptive software testing in the context of software cybernetics. Inf. Softw. Technol. **44**(14), 841–855 (2002)
29. Mahdavi-Hezavehi, S., et al.: A systematic literature review on methods that handle multiple quality attributes in architecture-based self-adaptive systems. Inf. Softw. Technol. **90**, 1–26 (2017)
30. Sculley, D., et al.: Hidden technical debt in machine learning systems. In: Proceedings of the 28th International Conference on Neural Information Processing Systems, pp. 2503–2511 (2015)
31. Humbatova, N., Jahangirova, G., Bavota, G., Riccio, V., Stocco, A., Tonella, P.: Taxonomy of real faults in deep learning systems. In: Proceedings of the 42nd International Conference on Software Engineering (2020)
32. Ammann, P., Offutt, J.: Introduction to Software Testing. Cambridge University Press, Cambridge (2016)
33. Felderer, M., Russo, B., Auer, F.: On testing data-intensive software systems. Security and Quality in Cyber-Physical Systems Engineering, pp. 129–148. Springer, Cham (2019). https://doi.org/10.1007/978-3-030-25312-7_6
34. Basili, V., Selby, R.: Comparing the effectiveness of software testing strategies. IEEE Trans. Softw. Eng. **SE–13**(12), 1278–1296 (1987)
35. Zhu, Q., Panichella, A., Zaidman, A.: A systematic literature review of how mutation testing supports quality assurance processes. Softw. Test. Verif. Reliab. **28**(6), e1675 (2018)
36. Erich, F., Amrit, C., Daneva, M.: A qualitative study of DevOps usage in practice. J. Softw. Evol. Process **29**(6), e1885 (2017)
37. Karamitsos, I., Albarhami, S., Apostolopoulos, C.: Applying DevOps practices of continuous automation for machine learning. Information **11**(7), 363 (2020)

Machine Learning Applications

Improving Quality of Code Review Datasets – Token-Based Feature Extraction Method

Miroslaw Staron[1]([⊠]) [iD], Wilhelm Meding[2], Ola Söder[3],
and Miroslaw Ochodek[4] [iD]

[1] Chalmers — University of Gothenburg, Gothenburg, Sweden
miroslaw.staron@gu.se
[2] Ericsson AB, Stockholm, Sweden
wilhelm.meding@ericsson.com
[3] Axis Communications, Lund, Sweden
ola.soder@axis.com
[4] Institute of Computing Science, Poznan University of Technology, Poznan, Poland
miroslaw.ochodek@cs.put.poznan.pl

Abstract. Machine learning is used increasingly frequent in software engineering to automate tasks and improve the speed and quality of software products. One of the areas where machine learning starts to be used is the analysis of software code. The goal of this paper is to evaluate a new method for creating machine learning feature vectors, based on the content of a line of code. We designed a new feature extraction algorithm and evaluated it in an industrial case study. Our results show that using the new feature extraction technique improves the overall performance in terms of MCC (Matthews Correlation Coefficient) by 0.39 – from 0.31 to 0.70, while reducing the precision by 0.05. The implications of this is that we can improve overall prediction accuracy for both true positives and true negatives significantly. This increases the trust in the predictions by the practitioners and contributes to its deeper adoption in practice.

1 Introduction

Machine learning algorithms are based on data in order to make predictions, recommendations and quantifications of entities. One of the areas where these techniques are used are source code analyses [17,29] or defect removal recommendations [10,21]. In this context, machine learning provides the possibility to process large amount of data (e.g. source code) without significant manual effort [22].

In our previous work, we used a novel way of characterizing software code – using the content of the lines of code or the code fragment (e.g. presence of variable declaration) rather than typical metrics (e.g. Chidamber-Kamerer Object-Oriented metrics [7,28]). This way of characterizing the code provides the possibility to capture the meaning of the code, which can be conceptually linked to classifications of the code, such as fault-proneness or coding guidelines' violations.

D. Winkler et al. (Eds.): SWQD 2021, LNBIP 404, pp. 81–93, 2021.
https://doi.org/10.1007/978-3-030-65854-0_7

However, the major challenges in extracting feature vectors from small fragments of code are that we cannot guarantee that the feature tranformation preserves the important aspects of the code fragment. In particular, that the extraction process results in an injective, but not surjective transformation, i.e. that two different lines have the same feature vector representation. An example of this situation is presented in Fig. 1 presents a situation when a software designer commented one line of code which contains a programming mistake. The comment is an important information in code classification as commented code is not relevant for the compiler and therefore not relevant for fault-proneness or code guidelines evaluation.

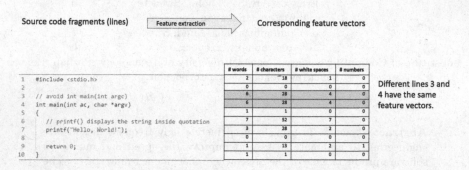

Fig. 1. Example of a typical feature extraction method, where two different lines have the same feature vector (lines 3 and 4).

The current ways of addressing this problem are to use predefined set of keywords or using statistic-based methods like Bag-of-Words [33] or even more advanced word embedding [9]. However, the statistical methods do not provide a guarantee that two different lines will have two different vector representations. Although in many cases this distinction is not required, there are applications where it is essential, for example when we want to predict which source code fragment violated a specific coding guideline, predicting which line can cause a specific test case to fail [2] or even counting lines based on specific patterns [18].

Therefore, in this paper, we address the following research question: *How to create a feature vector which quantifies software code based on its content preserving the equality relation between distinct code fragments?*

We search for an algorithm that can extract features based on the content of the code fragment (in this study it is a line), and that is an injective surjective transformation [8]. This property is important as the non-optimal quantification has a negative impact on the machine learning algorithms – if we cannot distinguish between two lines that are different, but have the same feature vectors, then we cannot guarantee that the data set is consistent. Two lines can be classified differently (e.g. one could be classified as violation and the other as non-violation), which can make the training of the machine learning algorithms difficult. The algorithms may not converge to an accurate model.

In order to create an algorithm that can be used in practice, we evaluate it in a case study of our industrial partner. At the company (Company A) we can analyze their proprietary software, developed and quality assured in a professional way. We used a similar approach as validating methods using design science or action research [3].

The results show that the new feature extraction method improves the performance of machine learning algorithms, in particular the Mathews Correlation Coefficient (MCC) from 0.31 to 0.70.

The remaining of the paper is structured as follows. Section 2 presents the most important related work. Section 3 presents the new feature extraction method. Section 4 describes our research design and Sect. 5 presents the results. Finally, Sect. 6 presents our conclusions, discussion and the further work.

2 Related Work

Traditionally, predicting the number of defects, their location or test case failures from source code properties is based on two different approaches. The first one is the usage of structural source code metrics and the second is based on static analysis of source code. There are meta-studies on defect predictions and the metrics used in the models [23, 26], showing that the field is still actively searching for the right metrics.

The use of structural code metrics has been studied extensively since the design of the object-oriented metric suite by Chidamber and Kemerer [6]. Studies by Basili et al. [4] presented evidence that these metrics are important in predictors for software defects, which was confirmed by later studies like Subramanyam and Krishnan [30]. Even recent advances in this field show that these metrics have effect on the software defects [19].

Although there are multiple studies where the structural metrics are used as predictors, there is no conclusive evidence which of these metrics are important and which are not. For example, a study by Tahir et al. [32] could not establish the relation between size, object-oriented metrics and software defects. The existing meta-analyses show that the size effect is an important confounding factor in all analyses – the larger the software, the more fault-prone it is (but also the larger the values of the metrics) [1].

In the area of static analysis, Nagappan and Ball [16] studied the use of static analysis metrics and tools as predictors for pre-release defects. The results showed that these kind of metrics can separate components into high and low quality ones. Studies in other domains show the same trend [12], which indicates that there is a relation between the properties of software code and the external properties of software, like its quality measured by the various defect-related metrics.

Schnappinger et al. [24] presented a study on the use of static analysis to predict maintainability of software, which our study builds on. We use similar methods for designing the machine learning classifier.

In addition to using different metrics to predict external properties of software, our work builds upon the advances of using machine learning in software analysis. Sultanow et al. [31] proposed a neural network to prioritize static analysis warnings in the context of continuous integration. We use a very similar classifier (neural network) in our work in order to minimize the confounding factors related to the choice of evaluation methods. In our previous studies we also established that using text analysis (Bag of Words) can successfully mimic static analysis [17].

Our study is a complement to the existing body of research as we use a novel way of analyzing the software code – we view the software code as a set of lines and tokens which have meanings that can be captured as feature vectors. We used a similar approach in our previous studies [2,18]. A similar approach was adopted by Shippey et al. [25], who used the information from the abstract syntax trees for as features. In our case, we use languages where the AST (Abstract Syntax Tree) is not available due to proprietary compilers and we focus on code fragments which are used in continuous integration. In that context, the fragments are often parts of functions, methods or classes and they cannot be compiled.

Finally, our work is important for the line of research of using textual features for source code analyses for maintainability and readability. For example Mi et al. [14] presented a study of how to improve readability of code using convolutional neural networks (although of a more complex architecture than ours). Xiao et al. [34] showed the use of word embeddings for finding the localization of defects in source code using LSTM models (Long-Short Term Memory), which is where we used the inspiration for including the LSTM layers in the design of our neural network. Although quite recent, this line of research has been shown to be quite promizing (e.g. [13]).

3   New Feature Extraction Method

The feature extraction algorithm is presented in Fig. 2[1]. It can be summarized in the following way. For each line, create a feature vector, check if the feature vector has already been found and check if the lines are the same. If not, then find which tokens differ these two lines and add one of these tokens to the set of features and start the process again. In this way, we have a guarantee that the feature vector representation of two distinct lines are different.

The algorithm starts with the initialization of the empty list and analyzing one line at a time (step 1 and 2). The analysis of the line, in step 3, uses an algorithm that creates a list of token based on the content from the file. The function that tokenizes the line uses whitespaces, commas, full stops and brackets as separators. We found that the following set of separators is optimal for such programming languages as C, C++, Python and Java: [, , /,(, |, ,),], {, }. In step 4 and 5 the algorithm adds a new token from the list and if there is no new token, then it takes one more line and looks for new tokens there. In step 6, the algorithm uses the list of features to check for features for each the each

---

[1] The full code of the featurizer can be found at: https://github.com/miroslawstaron/code_featurizer.

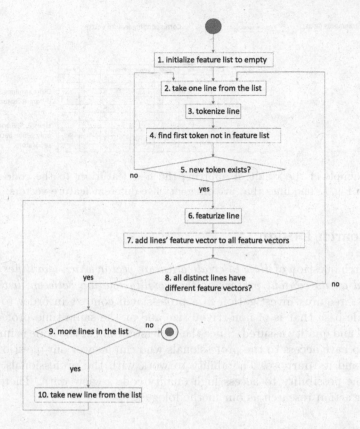

Fig. 2. Activity diagram presenting the algorithm for the new featurizer.

lines analyzed so far. Then it checks whether there are feature vectors that are identical and whether the corresponding lines are identical (step 8). In Fig. 2, the exit condition in step 9 is two fold – either the set of lines to featurize is empty or there are no new tokens to be added. The first condition is given, but the second is needed when the algorithm encounters lines that differ only in the number of whitespaces – e.g. "x = x + 1;" and "x = x+1" (spaces between x and 1).

Figure 3 presents the results of applying the new featurizer to the same code as in Fig. 1.

In the example in Fig. 3, lines 3 and 4 have different feature vectors. However, lines which contain only whitespaces or separators ({ and }), have feature vectors equal to all zeros, since we do not need this kind of lines in the analyses of the source code.

Although the size of the example is small, the full potential of the new featurizer is observed on larger data sets – code bases of over 10,000 lines of code. In these data sets, we need to find the right number of features as typical approaches result in the same feature vectors for two different lines.

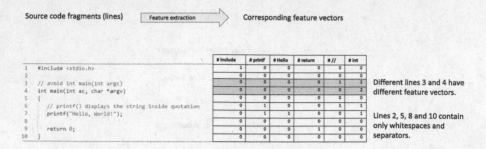

Fig. 3. Example of the result of applying the new featurizer to the code from the example in Fig. 1. The lines that are different have different feature vectors.

4   Research Design

The research question of *How to create a feature vector which quantifies software code based on its content preserving the equality relation between distinct code fragments?* requires investigation in a professional context in order to study a source code base that is of non-trivial size and at the same time professionally developed and quality assured. Since the understanding of the code is important, we need to have access to the professionals who can answer our questions about the code and its purpose. The ability to work with the professionals provides us with the possibility to access high quality code review data. Therefore, we settled for action research as our methodology [27].

4.1   Case Selection

In our case study we chose one company which develops embedded software products for the commercial market. The products are matured and the development team has over a decade of experience of agile software development and have been using continuous integration for over five years. We chose the company as it provided us with the possibility to analyze their code for software integration. The code is a mixture of Python and a proprietary integration language. This means that the code needs several pre-processing steps before it can be combined, which renders the static analysis and compiler-based approaches unusable in this context. From that perspective, we see the analysis of this code as the hardest scenario for automated analysis, which means that the we can generalize the results to the contexts which are simpler.

To evaluate the method, we benchmarked it to Bag-of-Words (BOW) feature extraction. Bag-of-words uses a vocabulary that can be either automatically extracted from the training examples or predefined. When the vocabulary is extracted from the training code it has to be passed as an input to the filter extracting features using BOW on the code to be evaluated. BOW counts the occurrences of tokens in the code that are in the vocabulary (the code is tokenized). Also, it can count occurrences of sequences of tokens called n-grams (e.g., bi-gram or tri-grams). N-grams are a valuable source of information for finding code guidelines violations since it is often important to understand the context in which a given token appears (e.g., `int a` vs. `class a`).

4.2 Data Collection

The code used in this study came from a development company for consumer products with embedded software. The studied organization, within this company, has over 100 developers who work according to Agile principles. They develop embedded software product, based on Linux and they adopted continuous integration for over five years ago.

The data for our analyses were collected from a code review system Gerrit [15]. This code review tool is designed on top of code management tool Git [5]. The tool provides the possibility for software designers to comment on the code from their peers and stop code of low quality to enter the main code branch. For our purposes, the tool provided us with the possibility to extract comments and make a sentiment analysis of the comments in order to classify the lines as "good quality" and "bad quality" – if a reaction was positive or negative respectively. Since the sentiment analysis is not the main purpose of this study, we used a simple, keyword based analysis of the comments. The process of extracting the lines, their classification and training the model is presented in Fig. 4.

4.3 Data Analysis

The model for the classifying the code to one of the classes was based on a convolutional neural network. The architecture of the neural network is presented in Fig. 5. The number of input parameters for the first layer is dependent on the number of features extracted. In the figure, the number is shown for the Bag-of-Word technique. The convolutional layers of the network use the window size of 5.

We chose this architecture as it provides the possibility to reduce the feature vector using convoluions. Since the new feature extraction vector resulted in large number of features (over 5,000), the convolutional neural network could reduce that number without the loss of information.

The size of the code base is presented in Fig. 6. The code base is not balanced when it comes to the two classes – correct code and code that reviewers reacted on, where the lines which were reacted upon positively are in majority.

In order to mitigate the problems related to the unbalanced classes, we used upsampling.

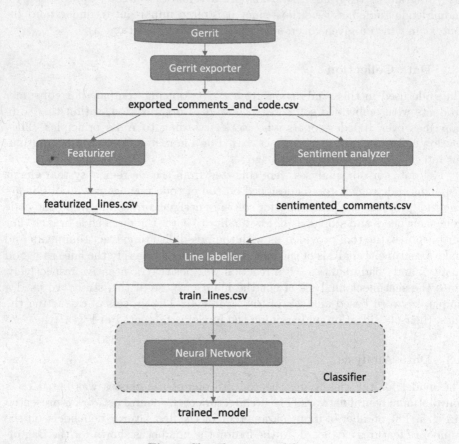

Fig. 4. Classification workflow.

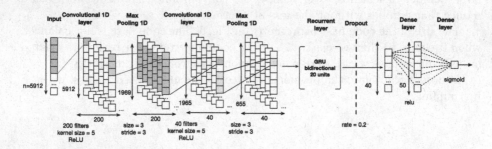

Fig. 5. Architecture of the neural network used for the classification task.

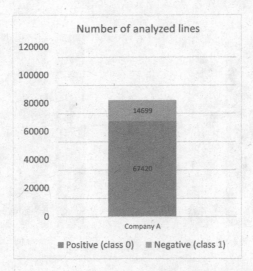

Fig. 6. Analyzed code bases for Company A and Company B; in each case, this is a subset of lines which were part of a review in the last few months.

The measures for comparing the performance of the machine learning algorithm for these two data sets are [20]:

1. Precision: the proportion of the predicted positive cases which are the real positive cases.
2. Recall: the proportion of real positive cases which are predicted as positive.
3. F1-score: the harmonic mean of precision and recall.
4. MCC (Matthews Correlation Coefficient): the measure describing the confusion matrix in a single number for binary classification problems.

The MCC measure is important as it is as close to a mean of the prediction measures for all classes as possible – both the true positives and true negatives are used in the calculations (compared to the measures for precision, recall and F1-score). It is also recommended for the evaluation of machine learning algorithms in software engineering [11].

5   Results

Figure 7 shows the summary of the evaluation measures for the code from Company A.

The difference between the two feature extraction techniques shows mostly in the value of MCC. The Bag-of-Words technique has a higher precision, but the overall measure (MCC) is worse in comparison with the new featurize extraction method.

This means that the BOW data set results in the predictors which favors one of the classes – the true positive cases. The new featurizer method results in the predictor which balances both the true positives and true negative cases.

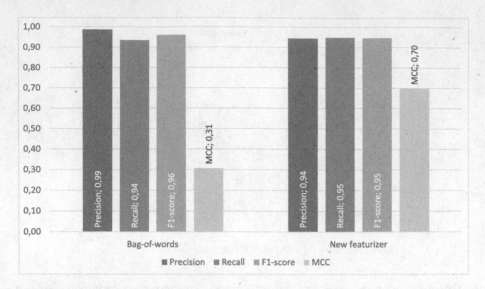

Fig. 7. Summary of the performance measures for two featurizers. Data set is code for Company A.

In the domain of the problem, i.e. finding which lines of code cause negative reactions of the code reviewers, this means that the predictor trained on the new featurizer data set provides fewer false positives. In comparison to the BOW-based predictor, the predictor provides a better overall performance.

6   Conclusions

Extracting features from software source code determines the ability to analyze the code using machine learning algorithms. Techniques available today provide rudimentary ways of extracting the features, but they are based on techniques used for either natural language analysis or they require compiling of source code. However, in the context of continuous integration, when source code is commited in fragments, the compilation process is not possible during the review of the source code by software designers.

Therefore, in this paper, we set off to address the research problem of how to create a feature vector which quantifies software code based on its content preserving the equality relation between distinct code fragments. We developed an algorithm which is based on the actual tokens used in the program code that is analyzed.

We used a neural network to train a predictor for the code quality based on a real-world scenario of code review analyses in continuous integration flow. The analyzed code was provided by our partner company and can be seen as one of the hardest cases as it is a mix of different programming languages and does not have a static analysis tool provided.

The results from our evaluations show that we could increase the overall accuracy of the predictions measured as Matthews Correlation Coefficient (MCC). The increase was from 0.31 to 0.70, with the reduction of the performance in precision (by 0.05) and increase in recall (0.01).

References

1. Mamun, M.A.A., Berger, C., Hansson, J.: Effects of measurements on correlations of software code metrics. Empirical Softw. Eng. **24**(4), 2764–2818 (2019). https://doi.org/10.1007/s10664-019-09714-9
2. Al-Sabbagh, K., Staron, M., Hebig, R., Meding, W.: Predicting test case verdicts using textual analysis of commited code churns (2019)
3. Antinyan, V., Staron, M., Sandberg, A., Hansson, J.: Validating software measures using action research a method and industrial experiences. In: Proceedings of the 20th International Conference on Evaluation and Assessment in Software Engineering, p. 23. ACM (2016)
4. Basili, V.R., Briand, L.C., Melo, W.L.: A validation of object-oriented design metrics as quality indicators. IEEE Trans. Softw. Eng. **22**(10), 751–761 (1996)
5. Bird, C., Rigby, P.C., Barr, E.T., Hamilton, D.J., German, D.M., Devanbu, P.: The promises and perils of mining Git. In: 2009 6th IEEE International Working Conference on Mining Software Repositories, pp. 1–10. IEEE (2009)
6. Chidamber, S.R., Kemerer, C.F.: Towards a metrics suite for object oriented design (1991)
7. Chidamber, S.R., Kemerer, C.F.: A metrics suite for object oriented design. IEEE Trans. Softw. Eng. **20**(6), 476–493 (1994)
8. Fenton, N., Bieman, J.: Software Metrics: A Rigorous and Practical Approach. CRC Press, Boca Raton (2014)
9. Goldberg, Y., Levy, O.: word2vec explained: deriving Mikolov et al'.s negative-sampling word-embedding method. arXiv preprint arXiv:1402.3722 (2014)
10. Halali, S., Staron, M., Ochodek, M., Meding, W.: Improving defect localization by classifying the affected asset using machine learning. In: Winkler, D., Biffl, S., Bergsmann, J. (eds.) SWQD 2019. LNBIP, vol. 338, pp. 106–122. Springer, Cham (2019). https://doi.org/10.1007/978-3-030-05767-1_8
11. Kitchenham, B.A., Pickard, L.M., MacDonell, S.G., Shepperd, M.J.: What accuracy statistics really measure. IEE Proc. Softw. **148**(3), 81–85 (2001)
12. Lindahl, T., Sagonas, K.: Detecting software defects in telecom applications through lightweight static analysis: a war story. In: Chin, W.-N. (ed.) APLAS 2004. LNCS, vol. 3302, pp. 91–106. Springer, Heidelberg (2004). https://doi.org/10.1007/978-3-540-30477-7_7
13. Liu, G., Lu, Y., Shi, K., Chang, J., Wei, X.: Convolutional neural networks-based locating relevant buggy code files for bug reports affected by data imbalance. IEEE Access **7**, 131304–131316 (2019)
14. Mi, Q., Keung, J., Xiao, Y., Mensah, S., Gao, Y.: Improving code readability classification using convolutional neural networks. Inf. Softw. Technol. **104**, 60–71 (2018)
15. Mukadam, M., Bird, C., Rigby, P.C.: Gerrit software code review data from android. In: 2013 10th Working Conference on Mining Software Repositories (MSR), pp. 45–48. IEEE (2013)

16. Nagappan, N., Ball, T.: Static analysis tools as early indicators of pre-release defect density. In: Proceedings of the 27th international conference on Software engineering, pp. 580–586. ACM (2005)

17. Ochodek, M., Hebig, R., Meding, W., Frost, G.: Recognizing lines of code violating company-specific coding guidelines using machine learning. Empirical Softw. Eng. **25**, 220–265 (2019)

18. Ochodek, M., Staron, M., Bargowski, D., Meding, W., Hebig, R.: Using machine learning to design a flexible loc counter. In: 2017 IEEE Workshop on Machine Learning Techniques for Software Quality Evaluation (MaLTeSQuE), pp. 14–20. IEEE (2017)

19. Ouellet, A., Badri, M.: Empirical analysis of object-oriented metrics and centrality measures for predicting fault-prone classes in object-oriented software. In: Piattini, M., Rupino da Cunha, P., García Rodríguez de Guzmán, I., Pérez-Castillo, R. (eds.) QUATIC 2019. CCIS, vol. 1010, pp. 129–143. Springer, Cham (2019). https://doi.org/10.1007/978-3-030-29238-6_10

20. Powers, D.M.: Evaluation: from precision, recall and F-measure to ROC, informedness, markedness and correlation (2011)

21. Rana, R., Staron, M.: Machine learning approach for quality assessment and prediction in large software organizations. In: 2015 6th IEEE International Conference on Software Engineering and Service Science (ICSESS), pp. 1098–1101. IEEE (2015)

22. Rana, R., Staron, M., Hansson, J., Nilsson, M., Meding, W.: A framework for adoption of machine learning in industry for software defect prediction. In: 2014 9th International Conference on Software Engineering and Applications (ICSOFT-EA), pp. 383–392. IEEE (2014)

23. Rathore, S.S., Kumar, S.: A study on software fault prediction techniques. Artif. Intell. Rev. **51**(2), 255–327 (2017). https://doi.org/10.1007/s10462-017-9563-5

24. Schnappinger, M., Osman, M.H., Pretschner, A., Fietzke, A.: Learning a classifier for prediction of maintainability based on static analysis tools. In: Proceedings of the 27th International Conference on Program Comprehension, pp. 243–248. IEEE Press (2019)

25. Shippey, T., Bowes, D., Hall, T.: Automatically identifying code features for software defect prediction: using AST N-Grams. Inf. Softw. Technol. **106**, 142–160 (2019)

26. Son, L.H., et al.: Empirical study of software defect prediction: a systematic mapping. Symmetry **11**(2), 212 (2019)

27. Staron, M.: Action Research in Software Engineering. Springer, Heidelberg (2020). https://doi.org/10.1007/978-3-030-32610-4

28. Staron, M., Kuzniarz, L., Thurn, C.: An empirical assessment of using stereotypes to improve reading techniques in software inspections. ACM SIGSOFT Softw. Eng. Notes **30**(4), 1–7 (2005)

29. Staron, M., Ochodek, M., Meding, W., Söder, O.: Using machine learning to identify code fragments for manual review. In: International Conference on Software Engineering and Advanced Applications, pp. 1–20. ACM (2020)

30. Subramanyam, R., Krishnan, M.S.: Empirical analysis of CK metrics for object-oriented design complexity: implications for software defects. IEEE Trans. Softw. Eng. **29**(4), 297–310 (2003)

31. Sultanow, E., Ullrich, A., Konopik, S., Vladova, G.: Machine learning based static code analysis for software quality assurance. In: 2018 Thirteenth International Conference on Digital Information Management (ICDIM), pp. 156–161. IEEE (2018)

32. Tahir, A., Bennin, K.E., MacDonell, S.G., Marsland, S.: Revisiting the size effect in software fault prediction models. In: Proceedings of the 12th ACM/IEEE International Symposium on Empirical Software Engineering and Measurement, p. 23. ACM (2018)
33. Wu, L., Hoi, S.C., Yu, N.: Semantics-preserving bag-of-words models and applications. IEEE Trans. Image Process. **19**(7), 1908–1920 (2010)
34. Xiao, Y., Keung, J., Bennin, K.E., Mi, Q.: Improving bug localization with word embedding and enhanced convolutional neural networks. Inf. Softw. Technol. **105**, 17–29 (2019)

Is Machine Learning Software Just Software: A Maintainability View

Tommi Mikkonen[1(✉)], Jukka K. Nurminen[1], Mikko Raatikainen[1],
Ilenia Fronza[2], Niko Mäkitalo[1], and Tomi Männistö[1]

[1] University of Helsinki, Helsinki, Finland
{tommi.mikkonen,jukka.k.nurminen,mikko.raatikainen,
niko.makitalo,tomi.mannisto}@helsinki.fi
[2] Free University of Bozen-Bolzano, Bolzano, Italy
Ilenia.Fronza@unibz.it

Abstract. Artificial intelligence (AI) and machine learning (ML) is becoming commonplace in numerous fields. As they are often embedded in the context of larger software systems, issues that are faced with software systems in general are also applicable to AI/ML. In this paper, we address ML systems and their characteristics in the light of software maintenance and its attributes, modularity, testability, reusability, analysability, and modifiability. To achieve this, we pinpoint similarities and differences between ML software and software as we traditionally understand it, and draw parallels as well as provide a programmer's view to ML at a general level, using the established software design principles as the starting point.

Keywords: Software engineering · Software maintenance · Artificial intelligence · Machine learning · Modularity · Reusability · Analysability · Modifiability · Testability

1 Introduction

Artificial intelligence (AI) and machine learning (ML) is becoming commonplace in numerous fields. Such techniques help us to build interactive digital assistants, plan our route in traffic, or perform stock transactions.

While there are several ways to implement AI features, for the purposes of this paper, we focus on ML, a flavor of AI where algorithms improve automatically through experience [12] particularly by approaches based on neural networks. Very large neural networks, commonly called deep learning, can have billions of parameters whose values are optimized during the training phase. The resulting trained networks are able, for example, to detect objects in pictures, understand natural language, or play games at a superhuman level.

With these ML features, a new challenge has emerged: how to integrate ML components into a large system? So far, we have found ways to build individual

D. Winkler et al. (Eds.): SWQD 2021, LNBIP 404, pp. 94–105, 2021.
https://doi.org/10.1007/978-3-030-65854-0_8

(sub)systems but there is little established engineering support for creating and maintaining large systems that should be always on, produce reliable and valid results, have reasonable response time and resource consumption, survive an extended lifetime, and, in general, always place humans first in the process. Since ML systems are built using software, we believe that these issues can only be mitigated by considering both software engineering and data science building ML software.

There are several overview papers about software engineering of ML applications. Reporting workshop results [7] discuss the impact of inaccuracy and imperfections of AI, system testing, issues in ML libraries, models, and frameworks. Furthermore, Arpteg et al. [1] identified challenges for software design by analyzing multiple deep learning projects. Some surveys have focused on particular aspects of software development, such as testing [15]. However, in comparison to most of the prior overviews, we take a more holistic system view, and structure the challenges brought by ML to qualities of software design, in particular in the context of software maintenance.

More specifically, we study ML systems and their features in the light of maintenance as defined in software product quality model standard ISO/IEC-25010 [6], and its five subcharacteristices (or attributes) – modularity, reusability, analysability, modifiability, testability. The work is motivated by our experiences in developing applications that include ML features as well as observations of others, in particular Google's machine learning crash course,[1] that points out that even if ML is at the core of an ML system, only 5% or less of the overall code of that total ML production system in terms of code lines. Our focus was on the characteristics of ML themselves; patterns, such as wrappers and harnesses, that can be used to embed them into bigger systems in a more robust fashion will be left for future work. Furthermore, in this work we explicitly focused on software maintainability, and other characteristics addressed by the standard are left for future work.

The rest of this paper is structured as follows. Section 2 discusses the background and motivation of this work. Section 3 then continues the discussion by presenting a programmer's view to AI. Section 4 studies maintainability of AI systems, and Sect. 5 provides an extended discussion and summary of our findings. Finally, Sect. 6 draws some final conclusions.

2 Background: ML Explained for Programmers

Machine learning is commonly divided into three separate classes. The most common is *supervised learning* where we have access to the data and to the "right answer" often called a label, e.g., a photo and the objects in the photo. In *unsupervised learning*, we just have the data and the ML systems try to find some common structure in the data, e.g., classify photos of cats and dogs to different categories. Finally, in *reinforcement learning* the system learns a sequence of

---

[1] https://developers.google.com/machine-learning/crash-course/production-ml-systems, accessed Aug. 18, 2020.

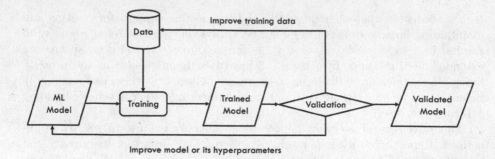

Fig. 1. Illustration of the ML training process and the search for a good model.

steps that leads it to a given goal, e.g., to a winning position in a game of chess. In this paper, we primarily deal with supervised learning, which is the most common approach. Many of our examples deal with neural networks although the ideas apply to other forms of supervised machine learning as well.

Developing an ML model requires multiple steps, which in industrial development are more complicated than in academic exploration [4]. Figure 1 gives an overview of the process. As the starting point, data must be available for training. There are various somewhat established ways of dividing the data to training, testing, and cross-validation sets. Then, an ML model has to be selected, together with the hyperparameters of the model. The hyperparameters define, e.g., how many and what kind of layers a neural network has and how many neurons there are in each layer.

Next, the model is trained with the training data. During the training phase, the weights of the neurons in the network are iteratively adjusted so that the output of the neural network has a good match with the "right answers" in the training material.

The trained model can then be validated with different data – although in software engineering this would more correspond to verification rather than validation that takes place with end users. If this validation is successful (with any criteria we decide to use) the model is ready for use. Then, it has to be embedded with the rest of the software system. Often the model, which can be the core of the application, is just a small part of the whole software system, so the interplay between the model and the rest of the software and context is essential [13].

To summarize, on the surface, the promise of ML systems is tempting for solving various problems. Based on the data only, the system learns to produce results without any human involvement or consideration. Internally, however, ML is just software and one way to think of deep learning is that it is just a new, yet very powerful, algorithm to the toolbox of the software developers. Its characteristics, however, are different from engineering tradition – instead of predefined executions, ML defines its own algorithms based on training data that is used to tailor the exact behavior, following the patterns that the system was able to absorb from the data.

So far, some work on the differences between AI software and "vanilla" software exist. In particular, Zhang et al. [15] refer to a number of challenges for AI testing: statistical nature of machine learning; data-driven programming paradigm with high sensitivity to data; evolving behavior; oracle problem; and emergent properties when considering the system as a whole. Moreover, the black-box nature of many ML approaches, especially neural networks, and the huge input space making the testing of rare cases difficult are common problems [10].

Next, we will elaborate the above challenges in the context of a real-life software project, and then we relate them to maintainability in terms of modularity, testability, reusability, analysability, and modifiability, as proposed by the ISO/IEC-25010 standard [6].

3 Challenges with an ML Component and Experiences from a Sample Project

In this section, we present a set of practical issues with an ML component that is concretized by a practical example. In this example research project[2] discussed in this paper, we worked with the Jira[3] issues tracking software. The Jira installation for managing the development and maintenance of a large industrial system contained over 120,000 Jira issues. Frequently, multiple (Jira) issues are about the same thing and should be *linked*: they can be duplicates, or otherwise related, such as an issue requiring the solution of another issue. As links are encoded manually in Jira, many may be missing. Because of the large number of issues, finding potentially missing links is hard. To help users to manage the links, we studied different natural language processing services based on existing algorithms and implementations to analyze the textual issue descriptions and to propose the users potentially missing links between them.

To summarize the experiences from the example, services that were promising in small scale or during development produced less good outcome in industrial scale use. There were also several challenges related to deployment, such as continuous integration and security, which are not covered here. In the end, rather than having one ML service that would produce the results, we used a design that combines the best results from different services and adds application-specific filters and contextualization. For a traditional software application, such design could have implied design flaws, but for AI software such design seemed a somewhat normal, i.e., things that one must be prepared to deal with.

While the example can be regarded as simple, it allows us to highlight detailed experiences, listed below in different subsections.

Stochastic Results. An ML model usually reaches certain accuracy, e.g., 98%. But how do we deal with the cases which are not correct? In classical software

---

[2] https://openreq.eu, accessed Aug. 18, 2020.
[3] https://www.atlassian.com/fi/software/jira, accessed Aug. 18, 2020.

we usually do not experience this at all. The problem gets even more complex when considering the different kinds of errors, for instance false positives against false negatives. The severity of errors is also system-specific.

Example: The detection of duplicates provides a score that can be used to filter and order expected true positives. However, users did not consider false positives, i.e., wrong proposals, a major problem when the results are ordered by the score. In this case the system only assists users leaving them the final decision and any help was considered beneficial. False negatives, i.e., not detecting duplicates, are more problematic.

High Sensitivity to Data. ML results are extremely sensitive to training data. A very minor change – even such as changing the order of two training examples – can change the system behavior. Similarly, any new training data will most likely change the outcome. Furthermore, measures such as accuracy and precision rely often on incomplete data, resulting in under- or overfitting due to, e.g., imperfect training data. Furthermore, operating in a dynamic environment of constantly changing data is challenging, because batch processing of data causes discontinuity and excessive resource consumption.

Example: Very careful fitting turned out to be unnecessary for the users and impossible because training data is always incomplete. The missing links, which we tried to detect, were also naturally largely missing from any available training data sample. We decided that better solution would be to monitor users' acceptance and rejection rates for the proposals.

Oracle Problem. In many cases where AI is involved, we do not know what is the right answer. This oracle problem is also common in the context of some algorithms, such as in optimization, where we do not know what is the best answer either. An additional aspect of this, related to AI ethics, is that we may have difficulty to agree what is the right answer [2]. A commonly used example of such a case is how a self-driving car should behave in a fatal emergency situation – to protect the persons inside the car or those around it, or, given a choice between a baby and an elderly person, which should be sacrificed.

Example: The users differ: one prefers to add many links while another uses links more scarcely. Likewise, if the issues are already linked indirectly via another issue, it is a subjective and context-dependent decision whether to add a redundant link. Thus, there are no single answers whether to add a link. Another challenge is that two issues can be first marked as duplicates but then they are changed and do not duplicate each other anymore.

Evolving Behavior. Many ML systems are build around the idea that the system can learn on-the-fly as it is being used. For instance, so-called reinforcement learning allows ML to chart the unknown solution space on the fly, aiming to maximize some utility function. The learning can also take place in operational use, meaning that the system can adapt to different situations by itself.

Example: All users decisions are anonymously recorded and the decisions can be used to change the behavior. However, when to change behavior? Changing behavior after each user might result in unbalanced behavior because decisions are subjective. Constant behavior change was also considered computationally expensive compared to its benefits.

Black Box. Neural networks are to a large degree regarded as black boxes. Therefore, understanding why they concluded something is difficult. Although there are new ways to somehow study the node activations in the network, it is still hard to get an understandable explanation. On one hand, this influences the trust users have to the system, and on the other hand, also makes debugging neural networks and their behavior very hard.

Example: Even in our simple case, the proposals do not provide any rational why a link is proposed so the users are not informed either. Without explanation and too many false positives – and perhaps even false negatives – users' trust and interest in the system in the long term remains a challenge.

Holistic Influences. With ML, it is not possible to pinpoint the error to a certain location in the software, but a more holistic view must be adopted. The reason why the classical approach of examining the logic of the computer execution does not work is that both the quality of entire training data set as well as the selected model have an influence. Consequently, there is no single location where to pinpoint the error in the design. As a result, a lot of the development work is trial-and-error to try to find a way how the system provides good results.

Example: It was not always clear should we improve data, model or software around it. Testing was largely manual requiring inspection and domain knowledge. We also tested another duplicate detection service but any larger data (more than 30 issues) crashed the service without explanation of the cause. As the results were similar with the first service, we quickly disregarded this service.

Unclear Bug/Feature Division. The division between a bug and a feature is not always clear. While it is possible there is a bug somewhere, a bad outcome can be a feature of the ML component caused by problems in the data (too little data, bad quality data, etc.). Some of the data related problems can be very hard to fix. For instance, if a problem is caused by shortage of training data it can take months to collect new data items. Moreover, even if the volume of data is large it can cover wrong cases. For example, in a system monitoring case, we typically have a lot of examples of the normal operation of a system but very few examples of those cases where something accidental happens.

Example: The Jira issues use very technical language and terminology, and can be very short and laconic. This caused sometimes incorrect outcome that is immediately evident for a user, e.g., by considering the issue, its creation time, and the part of software the issue concerns.

Huge Input Space. Thorough testing of an ML module is not possible in the same sense as it is possible to test classical software modules and to measure coverage. Thorough testing of classical software is as such also difficult but there are certain established ways, especially if the input space to a function/module is constrained. In an ML system, the input data often has so many different value combinations that there is no chance to try out them all or even to find border cases for more careful study. As shown in the adversarial attack examples, a small carefully planned change in input data can completely change the recognition of a picture or spoken command. In all cases we do not have nasty adversarial attackers but those examples show that such situations can happen if the data randomly happens to have certain characteristics.

Example: The Jira issues are very different from each other: Some of them are very short and laconic while others contain a lot of details. Sometimes the title contains the essential information while sometimes the title is very general and information is in the description. Thorough testing for optimal solutions, and even finding archetypal cases is hard.

4   ML in the Light of Maintainability

To study software maintenance in relation to ML software, the characteristics of ML systems were analyzed in the light of the key quality attributes. The analysis was first performed by two first authors, based on their experience on software design and ML, and then validated and refined by the rest of the authors.

Modularity. Modularity is the property of computer programs that measures the extent to which programs have been composed out of separate parts called modules. Module is generally defined to be a self-contained part of a system, which has a well-defined interface to the other parts, which do not need to care what takes place inside the module. The internal design of a module may be complex, but this is not relevant; once the module exists, it can easily be connected to or disconnected from the system.

In the sense of modularity, ML modules and classical SW modules coexist. Dependencies between modules may happen via large amounts of data, and output of an ML module can be input to another ML module. However, because the ML module operation is not perfect (e.g., accuracy 97%) modules taking output from ML modules need to live with partly incorrect data. When an upstream ML module is learning to be better, it is unclear what happens to downstream ML modules that have learned to deal with faulty input – when input now becomes more correct, will the downstream ML module actually give worse results? Oftentimes this implies that instead of decomposing complex ML function to simpler ones, the ML system is trained as a self-contained entity.

Another issue is related to interfaces. ML and especially neural networks are a bit too good to hide information. Therefore, understanding what is happening in an ML module is challenging and a lot of work on explainable AI is ongoing. Sometimes – as is the case in our example – dealing with this leads to using several modules that overlap in features for the best results.

Testability. Testing the software that implements machine learning can be tested like any other piece of software. Furthermore, the usual tools can be used to estimate the coverage and to produce other metrics. Hence, in the sense of code itself, testing ML software has little special challenges.

In contrast, testing ML systems with respect to features related to data and learning has several complications. To begin with, the results can be stochastic, statistical or evolving over time, which means that they, in general, are correct but there can also be errors. This is not a good match with classical software testing approaches, such as the V-model [11], where predestined, repeatable execution paths are expected. Moreover, the problems can be such that we do not know the correct answer – like in many games – or, worse still, us humans do not agree on the correct answer [2]. Finally, while many systems are assessed against accuracy, precision, or F-score using a test data set, there is less effort on validating that the test data set is correct and produces results that are not over- or underfitted.

In cases where the ML system mimics the human behavior – such as "find traffic sign in the picture" in object detection – a well-working AI system should produce predictable results. Again, most ML systems do not reach 100% accuracy so we need ways to deal with also inaccurate results. In some cases, like in targeted advertisement, it is adequate that the accuracy level is good enough while in other cases, like in autonomous vehicles, high trust to the results is necessary.

Reusability. Reusability is a quality characteristic closely associated with portability; it refers to the ability to use already existing pieces of software in other contexts. As already mentioned, in ML, the amount of code is relatively small and readily reusable, but reusing data or learning results is more difficult.

To begin with, there are reuse opportunities within the realm of ML itself. For instance, models can be reused. In fact, the present practice seems to be to pick a successful model from the literature and then try to use it – instead of inventing the models each time from scratch – even in completely different domains and use cases. Furthermore, the same data set can be used for training in several services, or one service can combine different data for training. For instance, in the example presented above, we used a number of different training data. Moreover, some data can be also quite generic, such as corpus from Wikipedia.

In ML, there is also a form of reuse called transfer learning [9]. In essence, transfer learning is an act of storing knowledge gained while solving one problem, and then applying the knowledge to a different but related problem at the level of trained ML modules. While the initial training often requires massive datasets, and huge amount of computing, retraining the module for particular data often requires far less data and computation. However, it may be hard to decide for sure if the retrained module is behaving well, because starting the training with a pretrained model can lead to rapid learning results, but this process does not guarantee much about its correct eventual behavior.

Finally, as ML modules can evolve over time, it is possible that they help to adapt the software to a new context. This can help reusing the modules in new applications.

Analysability. Since computer programs are frequently read by programmers while constructing, debugging, and modifying them, it is important that their behavior can be easily analyzed. Moreover, the behavior of neural networks can be studied and recorded for further analysis.

However, in ML, structural information associated with a neural network or characteristics of individual neurons bear little value in terms of analysability. Instead, the behavior is intimately related to data. Hence, while we can study individual neurons, for instance, the decision making process as a whole cannot be analysed without additional support in the system.

Modifiability. An ML module typically requires very little code. Therefore, modifying the logic of the ML module does not require much effort, and it seems that such code is modified somewhat routinely by the developers. There are also options to prune and shrink pre-trained networks so that they can be run with less hardware resources [14].

In contrast, modifying data can have dramatic effects. For instance, during training, a small change in input data – or just the change of the random generator seed – can change the results. Furthermore, the same training set can generate totally different neural network structure if we allow the system to search in an automated fashion – so-called AutoML [5] – for the best hyperparameters and network structure. As the neural network self-organizes itself, chances are that different instances trained with the same datasets organize themselves differently, so that their structures cannot be compared directly, and, worse still, produce partially different results.

The fact that different training data produces different results does not only introduce problems associated with modifiability. There can be cases where the only modification that is needed for using the same software is training with different data, and the software can be used intact.

5 Discussion

Above, we have presented a number of ML/AI related challenges to software maintenance. Table 1 presents the relationships between maintenance related characteristics and different aspects of machine learning. To summarize, software written for implementing ML related features can be treated as any other software from the maintainability perspective. However, when considering the data and the machine learning part, chances are that tools and techniques that are available are not enough. Therefore, in the end, the users should also be involved in the activities to ensure correct behavior.

Table 1. Summary of relationships between quality attributes and ML features.

	Modularity	Testability	Reusability	Analysability	Modifiability
SR	Neutral	Negative; testing aims to identify bugs, whereas stochastic results escape discrete testing	Neutral	Negative; stochastic results cannot be easily analyzed	Negative; modifying stochastic process can produce results that are hard to predict
HSD	Neutral	Negative; testing aims to identify bugs, and reliance to data does not lend itself to discrete testing.	Mixed; data sets can be reused, whereas reusing trained systems in different contexts can be hard	Negative; analysing data centric features often requires additional support from the infrastructure	Mixed; code can usually be modified with ease, whereas modifying data set can introduce complications
EB	Neutral	Negative; testing in general builds on discrete behaviors and faults, and has little room for evolving behavior	Mixed; evolving behaviors can adapt to new situations, whereas their validation and verification in a new context can be hard	Negative; analysing an evolving behavior is more complex than analyzing static behaviors	Mixed; the behavior can evolve to satisfy new needs, but triggering this can be complex
OP	Neutral	Negative; testing features whose output is not well defined is hard	Neutral	Negative; analysing an outcome that is based on foreseen results is hard	Neutral
BB	Positive; modules by default respect modular boundaries	Mixed; modules can be tested separately, but calculating metrics is hard	Positive; modules can be easily reused	Negative; the behavior is invisible and hence escapes analysis	Negative; black box behavior cannot be modified directly
HI	Negative; separation of concerns does not really happen as ML modules may be intertwined	Negative; testing cannot be focused but needs to be holistic	Negative; units of reuse are hard to define	Negative; holistic behavior is hard to analyze	Negative; modifications can have holistic effect
UD	Neutral	Negative; it is unclear when a test fails for what reason	Neutral	Negative; it is unclear what to analyze	Neutral
HIS	Negative; module with arbitrarily large input interface is difficult to manage	Negative; testing large input space is complex	Neutral	Negative; the larger the input space, the more complex analysis might be needed	Neutral

Legend:
SR: Stochastic results, HSD: High sensitivity to data, EB: Evolving behavior, OP: Oracle problem, BB: Black box, HI: Holistic influences, UD: Unclear bug/feature division, HIS: Huge input space

Threats to Validity. A key threat to the validity of our observations is that the study was performed by the authors based on their subjective experience on software design and maintenance, and ML systems. This can be a source of bias in the results. To mitigate this, all the results were analyzed by two or more authors as they were recorded in Table 1. A further threat to external validity is that there are various approaches to AI/ML, whose characteristics differ considerably. To mitigate this threat, we have narrowed the scope of this work to maintainability as defined by the ISO/IEC-25010 standard [6] and ML, which is only a subset of AI.

Future Work. As for future work, there are obvious directions where we can extend this work. To begin with, as already mentioned. We plan to perform a similar analysis of other software quality aspects of ISO/IEC-25010 standard. These include functional suitability, performance efficiency, compatibility, usability, reliability, security, and portability. While some of these are related to maintainablity addressed in this paper, these topics open new viewpoints to AI/ML software.

Furthermore, there are additional considerations, such as ethics [3], which have emerged in the context of AI. Such topics can also be approached from the wider software engineering viewpoint, not only from the perspective of novel techniques.

Finally, running constructive case studies on the impact of the software design principles in AI/ML software is one of the future paths of research. To disseminate the results, we plan to participate in the work of SO/IEC JTC 1/SC 42, which just accepted to start working on a working draft on "Software engineering: Systems and software Quality Requirements and Evaluation (SQuaRE) – Quality Model for AI-based systems".

6   Conclusions

In this paper, we have studied ML in the context of software maintainability. To summarize the results, while ML affects all characteristics of software maintenance, one source of complications is testing and testability of ML in general. Testing builds on the fact that software systems are deterministic, and it has long been realized that systems where different executions may differ – due to parallel executions for instance – often escape the traditional testing approaches. Same concerns arise when modules can have evolving behaviors or which can not be debugged with the tools we have. Hence, building new verification and validation tools that take into account the characteristics of ML are an important direction for future work.

To a degree, concerns that are associated with testability apply to analysability, including in particular black box behavior and reliance on large data sets. Hence, understanding how to measure test coverage or analyze the behavior of an AI module forms an obvious direction for future work. Moreover, since data is a key element in many ML systems, its characteristics will require special attention in the analysis.

Finally, as already mentioned as well as pointed out, e.g., by Kuwajima et al. [8], pattern-like solutions, such as wrappers, harnesses and workflows, for example, that can be used to embed ML related functions into bigger systems in a more robust fashion form a direction for future software engineering research.

References

1. Arpteg, A., Brinne, B., Crnkovic-Friis, L., Bosch, J.: Software engineering challenges of deep learning. In: Proceedings - 44th Euromicro Conference on Software Engineering and Advanced Applications, SEAA 2018. pp. 50–59. IEEE (2018). https://doi.org/10.1109/SEAA.2018.00018
2. Awad, E., et al.: The moral machine experiment. Nature **563**(7729), 59 (2018)
3. Bostrom, N., Yudkowsky, E.: The ethics of artificial intelligence. In: The Cambridge Handbook of Artificial Intelligence, vol. 1, pp. 316–334 (2014)
4. Breck, E., Polyzotis, N., Roy, S., Whang, S.E., Zinkevich, M.: Data infrastructure for machine learning. In: SysML Conference (2018)
5. Feurer, M., Klein, A., Eggensperger, K., Springenberg, J., Blum, M., Hutter, F.: Efficient and robust automated machine learning. In: Advances in Neural Information Processing Systems, pp. 2962–2970 (2015)
6. ISO: IEC25010: 2011 systems and software engineering-systems and software quality requirements and evaluation (SQuaRE)-system and software quality models (2011)
7. Khomh, F., Adams, B., Cheng, J., Fokaefs, M., Antoniol, G.: Software engineering for machine-learning applications: the road ahead. IEEE Softw. **35**(5), 81–84 (2018)
8. Kuwajima, H., Yasuoka, H., Nakae, T.: Engineering problems in machine learning systems. Mach. Learn. **109**(5), 1103–1126 (2020). https://doi.org/10.1007/s10994-020-05872-w
9. Pan, S.J., Yang, Q.: A survey on transfer learning. IEEE Trans. Knowl. Data Eng. **22**(10), 1345–1359 (2009)
10. Pei, K., Cao, Y., Yang, J., Jana, S.: DeepXplore: automated whitebox testing of deep learning systems. In: 26th Symposium on Operating Systems Principles, pp. 1–18 (2017)
11. Rook, P.: Controlling software projects. Softw. Eng. J. **1**(1), 7–16 (1986)
12. Schapire, R.E., Freund, Y.: Foundations of Machine Learning. MIT Press, Cambridge (2012)
13. Sculley, D., et al.: Hidden technical debt in machine learning systems. In: Advances in Neural Information Processing Systems, pp. 2503–2511 (2015)
14. Wang, H., Zhang, Q., Wang, Y., Hu, H.: Structured probabilistic pruning for convolutional neural network acceleration. arXiv:1709.06994 [cs.LG] (2017)
15. Zhang, J.M., Harman, M., Ma, L., Liu, Y.: Machine learning testing: survey, landscapes and horizons. IEEE Trans. Softw. Eng. arXiv:1906.10742 (2020). https://ieeexplore.ieee.org/document/9000651

Industry-Academia Collaboration

Solving Problems or Enabling Problem-Solving? from Purity in Empirical Software Engineering to Effective Co-production (Invited Keynote)

Tony Gorschek[1]([⊠]) and Daniel Mendez[1,2]

[1] Blekinge Institute of Technology, Karlskrona, Sweden
tony.gorschek@bth.se
[2] Fortiss GmbH, Munich, Germany

Abstract. Studying and collaborating with any software-intensive organization demands for excellence in empirical software engineering research. The ever-growing complexity and context-dependency of software products, however, demands for more pragmatic and solution-focused research. This is a great opportunity but it also conflicts with the traditional quest for "purity" in research and a very narrow focus of the work. In this short positioning, we elaborate on challenges which emerge from academia-industry collaborations and discuss touch upon pragmatic ways of approaching them along the co-production model which emerged from SERL Sweden.

1 Introduction

Software Engineering grew out of computer science-related fields and was baptized as a separate area to give legitimacy as a central discipline to handle challenges associated with the so-called software crisis becoming evident in the 1960s [8].[1] Empirical software engineering emerged in the 1990s and highlighted the focus on borrowing and adopting various types of empirical methods from other disciplines to conduct evidence-based research [6]. The aim was to collect evidence and build the bridge between practice in industry and research activities [1,8], thus, the discipline meant to increase the practical impact of mostly academic research contributions. The intent is explicitly stated in the name itself: "Empirical", denoting evidence collection and utilization, and "engineering" (-science) denoting the application of methods, tools, practices, and principles with the purpose of measuring the impact of said treatments in practice - this is also why many times the term "experimental" is intertwined with the "empirical" in empirical software engineering.

---

[1] http://homepages.cs.ncl.ac.uk/brian.randell/NATO/NATOReports/index.html.

© Springer Nature Switzerland AG 2021
D. Winkler et al. (Eds.): SWQD 2021, LNBIP 404, pp. 109–116, 2021.
https://doi.org/10.1007/978-3-030-65854-0_9

In this position paper, we introduce and discuss some of the main challenges associated with scientific work in the area of *empirical software engineering* – and possible ways forward. This is based on experiences and lessons learned from the immediate applied research environment of the Software Engineering Research Lab (SERL Sweden) at Blekinge Institute of Technology, its long-term research collaborations with industrial partners, as well as through its extended collaborations with and connections to relevant research and transfer institutes such as fortiss.

Hence, the context of the discussion in this manuscript, which lays out the foundation for the keynote at the Software Quality Days 2021, is not the product or invention or innovation itself, but it is rather the methods, models, practices, tools, frameworks, processes, and principles applied as a way to enable the repeatable engineering of software-intensive products and services – in short, "ways-of-working". In terms of engineering, we include the inception of a product, through the planning, design, and realization, as well as delivery and evolution until eventual decommissioning.

We will only be able to scratch the surfaces of new ways of working, but hope with this positioning to foster an overdue debate to challenge the purity of more "traditional" ways of empirical research in order to allow for a more productive co-production.

2   The Problem(s) with "Software"

The problems of the development of software-intensive products and services can be divided, as we argue, into three main categories. These categories in themselves shed light on the complexity of the field, both from an engineering perspective, but also from an engineering research perspective:

1. The inception phase is put under the same umbrella as the engineering of the product.
2. Human-centric activities are very hard to measure objectively.
3. Delivery of product/service is not seen as a cost or effort center as in manufacturing centric instances.

2.1   Inception and Engineering

In mechanical or electrical engineering, or in the design of complex systems studied in the area of systems engineering, the inception phase (where you would "invent" and conceptualize products with long market exploration or non-technical prototyping phases) is often not seen as part of the engineering itself. Think of circuit design, for example, or maybe even more apt, the creation of clay scale models of cars that are wrapped in foil to explore designs and engineering decisions by a car manufacturer. This is often seen as "creative" endeavors and not the engineering or production of the item itself. Further, post inception, there is a translation phase where the inception meets the reality (and the constraints) imposed by the engineering and production world – translating a raw concept into something that can be eventually produced taking into account cost, scale, and repeatability of quality. This school of thought treats both engineering and creativity as two isolated, distinct, and often competing islands.

In software engineering, in contrast, all these parts are seen as "development" and more importantly, these parts are counted and measured as part of the teams' work – ranging from first product or service ideas over the exploitation of requirements and the development of first prototypes to the development, quality assurance, and deployment. Even project management activities are found under the same umbrella we call software engineering. This has significant implications for many reasons, not least when comparing plan-outcome and looking into the efficiency of the engineering organization as compared to rather traditional fields [2]. Needless to say that the challenges faced in software engineering can often not be found in other engineering activities – simply because related sub-disciplines are not associated with the engineering itself: think of challenges in human-centred and inherently volatile sub-disciplines like requirements engineering or during inherently fuzzy and uncertain tasks such as effort estimations.

2.2 Human-Centric Activities

Since software is created by humans for humans, any metrics and measurements used are largely dependent on measuring people and measuring them indirectly via artifacts associated with those people; for instance, by counting defects and their severity. If we setting aside for a moment the ethical and social aspects of human-based metrics, measuring humans and their activities remains a very hard and error-prone task. Is one engineer mentoring another something really non-productive? In addition, metrics are very seldomly information bearers. Rather, they are indicators for further analyses. To give an example, context switching and its measurement can be a good tool to gauge, for instance, team independence and the ability to focus on tasks. However, using the metric as a stand-alone part can be fraught with peril. For example, trying to push down context switch might hamper coordination efforts between teams or the ability for experienced engineers to answer questions by less experienced ones. In a traditional production environment, you can measure waste (e.g., failures or material waste); however, what constitutes waste and how this is separated from overhead in more human-centered activities is complex and very much context-dependent. In the example with context switch – the "best" solution might not be to identify the phenomenon as Waste, rather as Overhead and that a balance of not too much and not too little needs to be found – if the balance is not maintained, Waste is introduced.

2.3 Delivery

First, most "software" developed is actually not stand-alone. Rather, it is part of a product or service. The old adage that "software is free to deliver" propagates the myth that delivering software is without cost. This is of course false.

To illustrate this, let us consider two extreme examples: A purely software-based product, such as accounting software, and an embedded software product, such an infotainment software in a car. In both cases, there is a significant cost for both the development company to package and supply (in essence commissioning) the product, and more importantly, there is a cost of risk for the customer. If consumers have accounting software that works well and that they use for their business, are they risk-averse in willingly updating the software as it might cause them harm (why fix what works?). On the other hand, the development company wants to push out a homogenous (and recent) version and variant of their product – if for no other reason to lessen their support costs and the costs of maintaining versions in the field. This might seem like a trivial part, but it has vast implications for development companies as the cost of product evolution, interoperability of features, but also products are affected by the version spread. An additional difference from traditional engineering (say a car manufacturer) is that the "development organization" in the case of software has to not only evolve the products but also continuously fix issues as they come along, likely in various versions and releases maintained in parallel (interrupting the work of evolution activities).

3   Research with and in Industry

The case for empirical software engineering, beyond data-collection activities, is that the contextual aspects of a company, domain, and development organization can be taken into consideration during research. This is especially true if the researcher uses a co-production approach to the research [3, 4, 10] as exemplified in Fig. 1.

Figure 1 gives an overview of a co-production model that evolved at SERL Sweden over the last decades with lessons learned from collaboration with over 50 industrial partners and two dozen research projects. The model should not be seen as a recipe or a blueprint to follow. It is rather an illustration of possible steps and aspects to take into consideration to realize close industrial collaboration from a research perspective.

Below, we elaborate each step and connect them to major challenges as well as opportunities we have experienced in above mentioned contexts. For details, please follow [4].

Starting the work with any company (industry partner) involves building trust as well as knowledge about the company and its domain [5], both from a contextual perspective, and the inner workings (steps 1–2). Finding proper problems before solving them properly is essential. For a researcher, however, this is also critical since it allows access and, more fundamentally, the building of trust, and the ability to identify sources and, more importantly, input as to how relevant data (to relevant problems) can be efficiently collected and how the data can and should subsequently be analyzed and interpreted. A critical part of the initial steps is to set realistic expectations. Especially in new relationships where companies are not used to researchers, industry partners may often fall to a default "consultancy" mindset. The main difference between consultancy and research from a research perspective is quite simply to follow the question whether there is anything new to accomplish. Research should, in our view, be

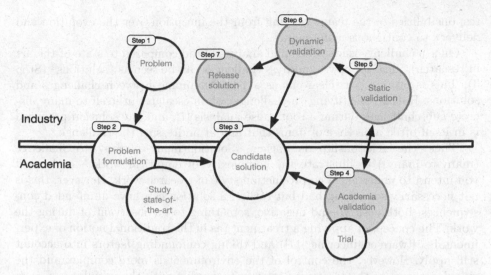

Fig. 1. SERL Co-production model. Adapted from [4].

characterized by that a new and relevant problem is solved, and/or new knowledge created (as the simplification of aiming for practical and/or theoretical impact). If this is not possible given a task, even partly, it should not be considered a viable piece of work that is equally relevant to both the participating researchers and practitioners. That being said, there are many types and flavours of research contributions. Say, for example, that a researcher aims at introducing already established (but new to their partner) ways of working. At a first glance, the researcher might not be creating new models, methods, practices, or equivalent. There might still be a research contribution as the introduction itself and the subsequent measurement of the effectiveness and efficiency of the proposed solution is a contribution. For the researcher, the trade-off is, however, the "researchabilty" of the work versus the effort put in versus the good-will created in the collaboration.

The main point here is to differentiate (steps 1–2) symptoms from actual challenge. "We have too many defects", as an example, can be a symptom of many things. Often addressing the symptom offers less researchability than addressing the underlying cause(es).

One of the main challenges here, in addition to selecting a challenge that is researchable, is that data collection often goes through people in a company, and often the measures are based on people. Setting aside ethical implications, which must be handled professionally, trust is paramount for access and to minimize the impact of the measurements. In this article, we do not even try to elaborate on this further to the extent it deserves. What is interesting to observe though is that the complexity of the case studied is compounded by both the human-centric part (as one often does not have machines to study), and the wide area of responsibilities of the teams ranging from the inception over the evolution and delivery to continuous maintenance.

Once a challenge is identified and analyzed (and compared to state-of-the-art in research), ideas for how to address challenges can be seen as "solutions" (Step 3). This is often not as clear-cut as a 1-to-1 mapping between challenges and solutions. Rather, identifying "a challenge" often escalates in itself to many discrete sub-challenges during a root cause analysis [7], and any solution proposed is in itself often a package of items that aim at addressing the challenge.

Thus the relationship is rather (Solution(many-to-many)-to-Challenge (many-to-many)) to illustrate the complexity of empirical work – at least if you intend to undertake a co-production style of research work. However, this is not necessarily something bad but rather, a solution can have unintended consequences, both positive and negative, something to be observant of during the work. The concept of applying a treatment (as in the traditional notion of experimental software engineering [11]) and taking confounding factors into account still apply. However, the control of the environment is more complex and the singular nature of the treatment is often in conflict with the usefulness of it in the case company.

Steps 4–6 should not be seen as validation only, even if their base purpose is to measure to what extent a solution impacts the company and solves the challenge(s) addressed; e.g. through a study where we aim at analyzing the extent to which we satisfied the original improvement goals. The base idea is to measure the effectiveness (fit for purpose) and the efficiency (fit for purpose in relation to cost) of a solution. An important part here which makes measurement more complicated is that every round of "validation" gives not only efficiency and effectiveness data, but also input as how the treatment (solution) can be improved to maybe give better efficiency and effectiveness. In essence, if we use this data to improve the solution as validation progresses, we make results between measurements harder to compare, and we potentially introduce confounding factors. So is the solution to keep the solution singular and pure throughout validation rounds? From a non-co-production perspective this would be best. However, from a practical perspective – if we want to continue collaborating with the company – this might not be the best or most desirable way.

These effects are impossible to remove completely, but they can at least be partly mitigated. Examples of mitigation are the selection of challenge-solutions. Smaller and faster iterations and interactions are not going to escalate in complexity as larger ones. In addition, a close collaboration beyond "data collection" is of utmost importance, in essence by adapting an action research approach [9] but only from a macro level perspective. That is to say, every step (e.g. a validation) can be conducted using any research method, e.g. via interviews, task observations, or by measuring results from tasks, just to name a few. Hence, our experience does not indicate that researchers should be involved in the actual application of the solution on a daily basis, as it is typically the case in action research, but, rather, that the close nature of introducing, training, monitoring, and measuring its application on a macro level is close to so called action research. This allows the researcher to catch contextual information as to how the solution is used, which are hard to measure, and/or even being able to catch if actions during solution validation invalidate measures that from an outside perspective look valid.

4   Discussion

What do the perspectives of inception-realization, human-centric and, and delivery have to do with the research? Studying and collaborating with any organization – (software) engineering research mandates empirical and collaborative activities – is both qualified and complicated by the contextual factors in question.

In this short position paper, we illustrated that not only are software-intensive companies not simpler than traditional ones, rather more complicated as the division of responsibilities are often less clear cut. Further, more "traditional" companies are not a reality anymore as most companies are becoming more and more software-intensive. Hence, the need for good, pragmatic, solution-focused research is growing exponentially. This is a great opportunity but also conflicts with the traditional quest for "purity" in research and a very narrow focus of the work. This can not be completely solved, but it is a balance that has to be struck out of necessity for the research to be credible and useful for the company.

This is important to understand for conveying how empirical work in software engineering is generally done, and how co-production style research should be approached in particular. We illustrated this along our co-production model which emerged from decades of academia-industry collaborations at SERL Sweden.

References

1. Basili, V.R., Selby, R.W., Hutchens, D.H.: Experimentation in software engineering. IEEE Trans. Softw. Eng. **7**, 733–743 (1986)
2. Gorschek, T.: Evolution toward soft(er) products. Commun. ACM **61**(3), 78–84 (2018)
3. Gorschek, T., Garre, P., Larsson, S., Wohlin, C.: A model for technology transfer in practice. IEEE Softw. **23**(6), 88–95 (2006)
4. Gorschek, T., Wnuk, K.: Third generation industrial co-production in software engineering. Contemporary Empirical Methods in Software Engineering, pp. 503–525. Springer, Cham (2020). https://doi.org/10.1007/978-3-030-32489-6_18
5. Junker, M., et al.: Principles and a process for successful industry cooperation-the case of TUM and Munich Re. In: 2015 IEEE/ACM 2nd International Workshop on Software Engineering Research and Industrial Practice, pp. 50–53. IEEE (2015)
6. Mendez, D., Passoth, J.H.: Empirical software engineering: from discipline to interdiscipline. J. Syst. Softw. **148**, 170–179 (2019)
7. Pernstål, J., Feldt, R., Gorschek, T., Florén, D.: FLEX-RCA: a lean-based method for root cause analysis in software process improvement. Softw. Qual. J. **27**(1), 389–428 (2019)

8. Randell, B.: The 1968/69 NATO Software Engineering Reports. History of Software Engineering 37 (1996)
9. Wieringa, R., Moralı, A.: Technical action research as a validation method in information systems design science. In: Peffers, K., Rothenberger, M., Kuechler, B. (eds.) DESRIST 2012. LNCS, vol. 7286, pp. 220–238. Springer, Heidelberg (2012). https://doi.org/10.1007/978-3-642-29863-9_17
10. Wohlin, C., et al.: The success factors powering industry-academia collaboration. IEEE Softw. **29**(2), 67–73 (2011)
11. Wohlin, C., Runeson, P., Höst, M., Ohlsson, M.C., Regnell, B., Wesslén, A.: Experimentation in Software Engineering. Springer Science & Business Media, Heidelberg (2012). https://doi.org/10.1007/978-3-642-29044-2

Experimentation in Software
Engineering

An Empirical Study of User Story Quality and Its Impact on Open Source Project Performance

Ezequiel Scott[✉], Tanel Tõemets, and Dietmar Pfahl

Institute of Computer Science, University of Tartu, Narva mnt 18,
51009 Tartu, Estonia
{ezequiel.scott,dietmar.pfahl}@ut.ee,
tanel.toemets@gmail.com

Abstract. When software development teams apply Agile Software Development practices, they commonly express their requirements as User Stories. We aim to study the quality of User Stories and its evolution over time. Firstly, we develop a method to automatically monitor the quality of User Stories. Secondly, we investigate the relationship between User Story quality and project performance measures such as the number of reported bugs and the occurrence of rework and delays. We measure User Story quality with the help of a recently published quality framework and tool, Automatic Quality User Story Artisan (AQUSA). For our empirical work, we use six agile open source software projects. We apply time series analysis and use the Windowed Time Lagged Cross Correlation (WTLCC) method. Our results indicate that automatic User Story quality monitoring is feasible and may result in various distinct dynamic evolution patterns. In addition, we found the following relationship patterns between User Story quality and the software development aspects. A decrease/increase in User Story quality scores is associated with (i) a decrease/increase of the number of bugs after 1–13 weeks in short-medium projects, and 12 weeks in longer ones, (ii) an increase in rework frequency after 18–28, 8–15, and 1–3 weeks for long, medium, and short projects, respectively, and (iii) an increase in delayed issues after 7–20, 8–11, and 1–3 weeks for long, medium, and short duration projects.

Keywords: User story · Agile software development · Quality assurance · Time series analysis · AQUSA · QUS · WTLCC

1 Introduction

Correctly defining and understanding what a software system is supposed to do is vital to any software project's success. Poor quality of software requirements has a severe effect on software projects success. It is widely known that requirement errors found in the later phase of the software development process cost

© Springer Nature Switzerland AG 2021
D. Winkler et al. (Eds.): SWQD 2021, LNBIP 404, pp. 119–138, 2021.
https://doi.org/10.1007/978-3-030-65854-0_10

significantly more than faults found early, during the requirements engineering. Low-quality requirements often cause the projects to exceed deadlines, increase the amount of rework and product defects [1]. In addition, ensuring high-quality requirements can be challenging as it is difficult to track and measure automatically [2].

To minimize the risk of communication errors as a potential threat to project success, requirements may be described using structured natural language (e.g., use case descriptions) or formal specifications. The downside of these methods is their high definition and maintenance cost.

Agile Software Development (ASD) methods recommend writing requirements in the form of User Stories as a possible solution that helps to save time by avoiding excessively detailed requirement documentation and to avoid that the focus is taken away from the actual software development task [3].

User Stories describe requirements as short texts with a strict structure consisting of three elements: (i) a desired function or property of the software, (ii) the stakeholder who requires this function or property, (iii) and the benefit of having this function or property. The most widely known template for writing User Stories was popularized by Mike Cohn [3] and proposes the following syntax: "As a <role>, I want <goal>, [so that <benefit>]".

The high interest in research on ASD [4] as well as the ever growing popularity of ASD as the development method of choice among software developers has been confirmed in several studies [5,6]. Since User Stories were introduced, they have become a popular method for capturing requirements in ASD projects [5,7,8], because software developers find them effective and useful [9].

While User Stories have a well-defined structure, they are still written using natural language and, thus, their quality may vary. The consideration of quality criteria, such as the INVEST criteria (independent, negotiable, valuable, estimable, small, testable) seems to have a positive effect on software developers' attitudes towards User Stories, as they believe that using User Stories increases productivity and quality [10]. However, there exists little empirical evidence confirming the existence of such an effect in practice [9].

Our study aims to shed light on two research questions. Firstly, we analyze the evolution of User Story quality over time for the purpose of monitoring. Secondly, we investigate the relationships between User Story quality and characteristics of the development process, i.e., rework and delay, as well as the product, i.e., software quality. We conduct an empirical study on the data collected from six open-source software projects. To assess the quality of User Stories we apply the Quality User Story (QUS) framework together with the Automatic Quality User Story Artisan (AQUSA) open source software tool [11]. We are not only interested in finding out whether there exists an effect of User Story quality on process and product properties. We also try to find out whether it is possible to predict with how much delay a change of User Story quality in one sprint has an effect on process and product properties in later sprints. Our results indicate that a decrease in User Story quality scores seems to be associated with an increase of the number of bugs after 6 and 12 weeks in short and large projects, respectively; an increase in rework frequency after 1 and 8 weeks in short and large projects, respectively; and an increased number of delayed issues after 1 and 10 days in short and large projects, respectively.

The rest of our paper is structured as follows. In Sect. 2, we present related work. In Sect. 3, we introduce the research questions and describe the research design of our study. In Sect. 4, we present the results. In Sect. 5, we discuss our results and limitations of the study. In Sect. 6, we conclude the paper.

2   Related Work

2.1   Quality of User Stories

Several approaches exist for measuring the quality of User Stories. Literature covering this field are quite recent which shows the growing interest of the topic and its relevance in the current software engineering research. As stated in a recent study by Lucassen et al. [9], proprietary guidelines or the application of the INVEST criteria [10] are the most popular approaches used for assessing User Stories. Buglione and Abran [12] point out that User Stories without enough level of detail or incomplete User Stories can be the cause of incorrect effort estimation. Therefore, they highlight the importance of applying INVEST guidelines in order to reduce estimation error caused by low-quality User Stories. While the INVEST characteristics seem to be comprehensive, they are difficult to measure. Therefore, Lucassen et al. [11] developed the QUS framework supported by the AQUSA software. Since we used these instruments in our study, more detail is provided when we describe our research design in Sect. 3.

Lai proposes the User Story Quality Measurement (USQM) model [13]. This model is more complex than the INVEST model and organizes User Story quality metrics in three layers. Layer "Discussable and Estimable Quality" consists of "Clarity Contents", "Low Complexity", and "Modularity". Layer "Controllable and Manageable Quality" consists of "CM System", "Version control tools", and "Cross-reference Table". The third and last layer "Confirmable quality" consists of "Assured Contents", "Testability", and "Verifiability". Since there doesn't seem to exist tool support for automatic measurement of criteria in the USQM model, the model is difficult to apply.

To solve issues originating from the fact that User Stories are written using natural language, de Souza et al. [14] propose the use of domain ontologies. This is expected to improve the quality of User Stories as it removes ambiguity. This approach, however, has not yet been evaluated much in practice.

2.2   Empirical Studies on the Impact of Requirements Quality

Firesmith [1] described twelve requirement engineering problems and their causes based on practical experience gathered while working with numerous real-life projects. He states that an increase in the number of defects and delays can be caused by numerous sub-problems, which in turn might root in problems like poor requirement quality, requirements volatility, or an inadequate requirements engineering process.

Rodríguez-Pérez et al. [15] studied the causes of bugs based on project data. They propose a model that groups bugs into two categories, intrinsic and extrinsic bugs. Intrinsic bugs are introduced by changes in the source code. Extrinsic bugs are introduced by requirement changes or other issues not recorded in the source code management system. The authors also state that an important limitation of their model is that it does not cover bugs caused by faulty requirements in the first place. Therefore, this model is not used in our study.

Sedano et al. [16] conducted a participant-observation study about waste in software development. The authors observed eight projects and conducted interviews with project team members. As a result, they established an empirical waste taxonomy listing nine types of software waste. As a possible cause of rework waste the authors identified requirement problems, more precisely User Stories without concrete complete criteria or rejected User Stories.

Tamai et al. [17] examined 32 projects to explore the connection between requirements quality and project success. A key finding was that requirements specifications were poor in those projects where significant delays happened.

The creators of the QUS framework and AQUSA tool evaluated their framework in a multi-case study involving three companies [11]. The purpose of the study was to explore whether their framework and tool affects the work of software developers positively. Thirty practitioners used the QUS framework and AQUSA tool for two months. With the help of surveys and interviews, the authors collected data for the following metrics at the start and during the case study: User Story quality, perceived impact on work practice, amount of formal communication, rework, pre-release defects, post-release defects, and team productivity. The authors found that the quality of User Stories improved over time after introduction of the QUS framework but they were not able to find clear evidence about an effect on the other metrics. The authors conclude that more data should be collected and they encourage others to conduct similar studies to identify the effects of User Story quality on the software development process and its outcomes.

2.3   Time Series Analysis in Software Engineering

Time series methods have been used for different purposes in software engineering. For example, Jahanshahi et al. [18] conducted time series analysis with the ARIMA (Auto Regressive Integrated Moving Average) model to predict the number of anomalies in software. Kai et al. [19] describe the usage of time series analysis for identifying normal network traffic behaviour. In a paper by Herraiz et al. [20] time series analysis is used for forecasting the number of changes in Eclipse projects. A recent paper by Choras et al. [21] explores the possibilities for predicting software faults and software quality by using time series methods. In their study, the authors compared the ARIMA, Random walk, and Holt-Winters forecast models with ARIMA showing the best performance. The models were tested with data on sprint backlog size, number of tasks in progress, and number of delayed tasks. Choras et al. also state that automated quality analysis is important for managerial roles like team leaders and product owners as it helps them make informed decisions regarding project timing, quality prediction, and other important aspects. For the purpose of correlation analysis between time-series, the Windowed Time Lagged Cross Correlation (WTLCC) method [22] has been proposed. This is the method we use in our study.

2.4 Summary

In summary it can be said that poor quality of requirements quality can be related to various issues such as increased number of defects, and excessive rework and delay. As stated by Choras et al. [21], automated quality related analysis is important for team leaders, product owners, and other similar roles for monitoring the software development process and for making informed decisions. Regarding User Stories various approaches have been used to improve and measure their quality but these approaches have not yet been applied on larger data sets to forecast User Story quality for the purpose of monitoring. In addition, the relationship between User Stories quality the amount of quality problems, delays, and rework has not yet been studied extensively.

3 Study Design

An overview of our study design is shown in Fig. 1. We start with acquiring data from several publicly available JIRA server instances. The data is collected from real-life open source ASD projects. In order to understand the data, a significant amount of data exploration, data pre-processing and data cleaning steps are applied to make the data ready for analysis. Once the dataset has been cleaned, the User Stories are selected and their quality measured with the help of the AQUSA tool. As a result, a list of defects related to the User Stories is obtained and the quality score calculated based on those defects. We also calculate the software development performance measures from the dataset, i.e., number of issues labeled as "bug", frequency of rework occurrence, and frequency of delay occurrence. The quality scores and performance measures are captured as time series and their correlations analyzed using Window Time Lag Cross Correlation (WTLCC).

3.1 Research Questions

Our study tackles two research questions, RQ1 and RQ2. RQ1 focuses on exploring how the quality of User Stories changes over time and whether this can be monitored automatically. RQ1 is formulated as follows:

RQ1: What dynamic patterns can be observed when applying automatic measurement of User Story quality for the purpose of monitoring?

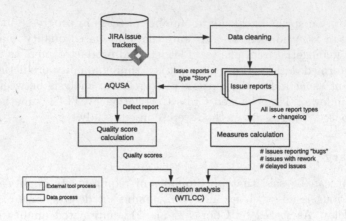

Fig. 1. Conceptual scheme of the study design.

To answer RQ1, we rely on the QUS framework along with the AQUSA tool. In order to express User Story quality with one number, we introduce a formula that maps the data collected by the AQUSA to a rational number in the interval [0, 1]. With the automatic monitoring of User Story quality in place, we study the relationship between User Story quality and three external quality characteristics of open-source ASD projects, i.e., number of bugs (issues labeled as "Bug"), rework done (re-opened issues of all types), and delays (issues not closed on due date). RQ2 is formulated as follows:

RQ2: What is the relationship between the quality of User Stories and other aspects of software development? The aspects studied are number of bugs, rework done (re-opened issues), and delays (based on due date).

Regarding the relationship between User Story quality and number of bugs, we expect that poorly written User Stories affect the understanding of requirements negatively and, therefore, increase the number of bugs found in testing or by end users. Similarly, we expect that poorly written User Stories increase the amount of rework done and the number of delays.

To answer RQ2, time series data of User Story quality, number of bugs, rework and delays is collected. In the rare case of missing values we use imputing methods. For the correlation analysis, we apply the Windowed Time Lagged Cross Correlation (WTLCC) method [22].

3.2   Initial Dataset

We collected data from open-source projects using JIRA, a popular software development project management tool. Our initial dataset consisted of issue reports and their change logs from ten open-source ASD projects. Of them, eight projects had already been used in previous studies [23–25]. We identified two additional projects for our study and collected the relevant data.

Our initial dataset contained projects from different domains and with variance regarding the number of issues, developer experience, and development period. The original dataset had more than 20K issue reports.

3.3   Data Cleaning

We applied several steps for cleaning the collected dataset. First, we kept issue reports of type "Story" for calculating the quality of user stories, issue reports of type "Bug" for calculating the number of bugs, and issue reports of type "Task" for calculating the occurrences of rework and delay. We only considered issue reports in complete status, indicated by the tags "Closed", "Done", "Resolved", and "Complete".

During the exploratory data analysis, we found that projects used different Jira fields to store the textual description of a User Story. Some projects used the field "Summary" whereas others used the field "Description". After evaluating several alternatives, we opted for keeping both fields and evaluated their quality separately.

We applied several cleaning steps to remove the noise from the dataset and avoid misleading conclusions. In total, we applied 16 cleaning steps including the removal of duplicates, empty data, and the cleaning of textual descriptions by removing hyperlinks, code snippets, among others. The complete list of cleaning steps is given in Appendix. After the cleaning, we found that several projects only have few user stories (less than 30) such as the projects MESOS, SLICE, NEXUS, and MULE. We excluded these projects from the analysis since these few data points can not reveal reliable patterns in the data. The resulting dataset consists of six projects. Table 1 describes the projects (after cleaning) considered in the analysis. We consider all projects as completed as the data was collected more than one year after the latest observed activity (24 Aug 2018, project COMPASS). Two of the projects, i.e., APSTUD and COMPASS have a relatively short duration (313 and 338 days, respectively). Two other projects, i.e., TIMOB and TISTUD, have a relatively long duration (1625 and 1295 days, respectively). The projects DNN and XD are inbetween (869 and 726 days, respectively).

Table 1. Descriptive statistics of the projects in the dataset.

Project	Stories	Bugs	Rework	Delays	Quality				Development period	
					Mean	Std	Min	Max	From	To
APSTUD	151	329	160	87	0.90	0.04	0.67	0.92	08.06.2011	14.06.2012
COMPASS	98	427	13	319	0.96	0.05	0.83	1.00	20.09.2017	24.08.2018
DNN	250	1075	524	679	0.90	0.06	0.67	1.00	29.07.2013	15.12.2015
TIMOB	255	1052	399	160	0.88	0.04	0.75	0.92	22.11.2011	05.04.2016
TISTUD	525	1380	792	567	0.90	0.03	0.75	0.92	01.03.2011	21.07.2014
XD	2135	476	124	251	0.90	0.03	0.67	1.00	12.04.2013	30.11.2015
Total	3414	4739	2012	2063	–	–	–	–	–	–
Median	252.5	764	279.50	285	0.90	0.04	0.71	0.96	–	–
Mean	569	789.83	335.33	343.83	0.91	0.04	0.72	0.96	–	–

Several projects had inactive development periods at the start or end of the project. We manually inspected the dataset regarding the number of issue reports created and we kept only the issues created during the active development periods.

3.4 Measurement

To study the variation of the quality of User Stories over time, we define a measure that quantifies the quality. To study the correlation between user story quality and project performance, we measure project performance by counting the number of bugs reported, the number of occurrences of rework, and the number of occurrences of delays to study.

Quality of User Stories (Q): For each issue tagged as "Story" we calculated the quality of the text contained in the fields "Summary" or "Description" based on the defect report generated by the AQUSA Tool. The tool implements the quality model QUS proposed by [11] and is publicly available[1]. The tool analyzes the descriptions of the User Stories and uses a linguistic parser to detect violations. As a result, the AQUSA tool reports each violation as a defect along with its type, i.e., kind and subkind, and its severity. There are three possible severity values, i.e., high, medium, and minor, and 13 possible defects in total. Table 2 shows the different types of defects that AQUSA can report.

Table 2. Possible defects from AQUSA

Kind	Subkind	Severity
well_formed	no_means	high
well_formed	no_role	high
unique	identical	high
minimal	brackets	high
minimal	indicator_repetition	high
atomic	conjunctions	high
well_formed_content	means	medium
well_formed_content	role	medium
well_formed	no_ends	medium
uniform	uniform	medium
well_formed	no_ends_comma	minor
well_formed	no_means_comma	minor
minimal	punctuation	minor

We use a local instance of the AQUSA tool to process the user stories in our dataset. Then, the report generated by AQUSA is processed to quantify the quality of each user story and get a numeric value between 0 and 1. The quality of a

---

[1] AQUSA Tool repository – https://github.com/gglucass/AQUSA.

user story Q is calculated as $Q = 1 - P$, where P is a penalty value calculated as a function of the number of defects and their severity. Equation 1 defines the formula to calculate the quality score of a given user story, where f_c is the percentage of defects of the user story in a category $c \in C$, $C = \{high, medium, minor\}$, and w'_c is the normalized weight for category c. To assign weights that correspond to the level of severity, we set $\mathbf{w'} = (0.5, 0.33, 0.16) = (\frac{3}{6}, \frac{2}{6}, \frac{1}{6})$ as a result of using $\mathbf{w} = (3, 2, 1)$ for high, medium, minor severity, respectively. The total number of defects possible in a severity category is 6 (high), 4 (medium), and 3 (minor), respectively.

$$Q = 1 - P = 1 - \sum_{c \in C} w'_c f_c \text{ with } w'_c = \frac{w_c}{\sum_{j=1}^{|C|} w_j} \text{ and } f_c = \frac{\#defects_c}{\#total\_defects_c} \quad (1)$$

Number of Bugs (B): Count of the issue reports of a project where the type is "Bug" and the status is complete (e.g. "Closed", "Done", "Resolved", or "Complete").

Rework (R): Count of the issue reports of a project that were re-opened. To calculate this, we analyze the log of changes of each issue. By default, JIRA records every change made to the issues along with a timestamp in a changelog. Therefore, if an issue was in status "Reopened", it is considered as rework.

Delays (D): Count of issue reports of a project that were completed after their originally planned date. To calculate this, we compare the issue resolution date with the end date of the sprint to which the issue was assigned to.

3.5 Data Analysis

We first create a time series representation for the quality of the user stories Q_p for each ASD project p in the dataset. We also create time series for bugs (B_p), issues with rework (R_p), and delayed issues (D_p). For indexing the time series, we use the issue creation date for user stories and bugs, the date when the change was made for rework, and the issue resolution date for delays. The data is re-sampled over 14 business days by using the mean and missing values are imputed by interpolation.

RQ1: To study the evolution of the quality of user stories over time, we present each time series Q_p in a separate plot and we describe the evolution of the quality by visual inspection.

RQ2: To study the relationship between the quality of the user stories Q_p and the variables of interest B_p, R_p, and D_p, we use Windowed Time Lag Cross-correlation (WTLCC). WTLCC is a method that allows us to study the association between two time series, $x(t)$ and $y(t)$ with $t = 1, 2, \ldots, T$, at different time lags (τ) and temporal changes in that association along the sample period [26,27]. Thus, for a window size of $W(W < T)$, a pair of windows $\mathbf{Wx}$ and $\mathbf{Wy}$ can be selected for two data vectors x and y respectively, and the cross-correlation between the windows (WTLCC) at time t for different time lags (τ)

is given by Eq. 2, where $\mu(\mathbf{Wx})$, $\mu(\mathbf{Wy})$, $\sigma(\mathbf{Wx})$ and $\sigma(\mathbf{Wy})$ are the means and standard deviations of the windows $\mathbf{Wx}$ and $\mathbf{Wy}$.

$$r_t(\mathbf{Wx}, \mathbf{Wy}, \tau) = \frac{1}{W - \tau} \sum_{i=1}^{W-\tau} \frac{(\mathbf{Wx}_i - \mu(\mathbf{Wx}))(\mathbf{Wy}_{i+\tau} - \mu(\mathbf{Wy}))}{\sigma(\mathbf{Wx})\sigma(\mathbf{Wy})} \tag{2}$$

The calculation of WTLCC involves the selection of the window size. To the best of our knowledge, there is no method to determine the window size and, therefore, the window size must be determined based on theoretical considerations or data characteristics. The window size also defines the desired level of granularity during the analysis. We did a preliminary exploration of the results using different window sizes such as monthly and quarterly time periods. We finally opted for splitting the entire development period into four equally-sized windows. This way, the resulting windows are easy to explain. The first window (window 0) may correspond to the set up of the project, the next two windows (window 1 and 2) represent the development phase where most of the features are developed, and the last window (window 3) refers to the project finalization phase.

The results are depicted using heatmaps, a visualization technique that helps us with the inspection of the results at different time lags. We interpret the correlation values (r) by following Cohen's guidelines [28], where small, medium, and large effect sizes are $0.1 \leq r < 0.3$, $0.3 \leq r < 0.5$, and $0.5 \leq r$, respectively.

When analyzing the heatmaps, we are mainly interested in high positive or negative correlations with positive lags. In general, we expect a negative correlation between user story quality and the variables of interest since we assume that an increase (decrease) of user story quality results in a decrease (increase) of the project performance (i.e., bug/rework/delay count) after some lag time.

Positive correlations could be difficult to explain. Why would, for example, an increase in user story quality correspond to an increase in the number of bugs after some delay? A possible explanation could be that the work triggered by the content of the user story is complex or difficult by nature and, thus, more prone to bugs. Another reason could be a technical effect of the choice of window size.

It is also possible to find correlations with negative lags. For example, an increase (decrease) of the number of bugs yields an increase (decrease) of user story quality after some lag time (delayed positive correlation). This could indicate that teams have improved the quality of their user stories as a consequence of a previous increase in the number bugs. Or, in the reaction to less bugs, more time is spent on creating more user stories less carefully. Additional analyses would be needed to clarify this situations.

Finally, there is the possibility that, after some lag time, an increase (decrease) in bug count is followed by a decrease (increase) in user story quality (delayed negative correlation). This could be interpreted, for example, as a situation where, due to an increasing number of bugs, more time has to be spent on bug fixing and, thus, less time is available for writing proper user stories.

Conversely, less bugs (and therefore less rework effort) might give more time for thinking about the requirements resulting in better user story quality.

4   Results

4.1   Study Population

As presented in Table 1, our cleaned dataset contains six projects with 3414 user stories, 4739 bug reports, 2012 rework cases, and 2063 delays. The project COMPASS has the smallest number of user stories and rework whereas APSTUD has the smallest number of delays and bug reports. The project XD has the largest number of user stories. Overall, the median number of user stories, bugs, rework, and delays is 252, 764, 279, and 285, respectively.

Table 1 also shows the descriptive statistics of the quality of the user stories. Overall, TIMOB has the lowest quality values whereas COMPASS has the highest. The projects XD, TISTUD, APSTUD, and DNN also have good quality values as their mean quality value is 0.9. The projects have a low standard deviation value regarding their quality values (mean std = 0.04).

4.2   User Stories Quality Monitoring and Evolution Patterns

Figure 2 shows the evolution of the mean quality of user stories over time. These graphs are useful to show how the quality of user stories can be used for monitoring purposes. A quantitative measure of the quality of the user stories of each project can be calculated by applying Eq. 1 to the defect report created by AQUSA tool. Although the quality values remain almost stable due to the low standard deviation (see Table 1), it can be seen that the overall quality values vary over time exhibiting different patterns.

Figure 2 shows that project XD is rather stable since it has low variance. On the other hand, projects such as DNN and COMPASS exhibit an erratic behavior. Moreover, both projects show a trend of decreasing user story quality over time as it is shown by the regression line. The remaining projects indicate a slight increase of user story quality over time as their regression lines have a positive slope.

4.3   User Story Quality and Project Performance

Bug Count. Figure 3 shows the results of applying WTLCC analysis to the six projects. The heatmaps associate the quality of user stories with the number of bugs. In each heatmap, the values on the y-axis represent the labels of the four windows used in the analysis. The x-axis shows the lag in business days that is applied before matching user story quality with the number of bugs. The correlation values are represented by the color scale. The title shows the name of the project along with the number of business days analyzed (n) on each case since the correlation analysis requires that the series occur simultaneously and in similar lengths.

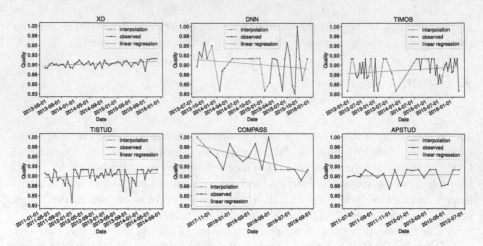

Fig. 2. Evolution of quality of user stories over time. A linear interpolation method was used to impute missing data points (red color) (Color figure online).

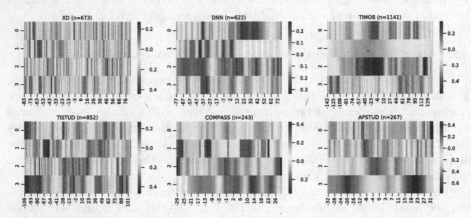

Fig. 3. Heatmaps representing the WTLCC results to compare the quality of user stories with the number of bugs.

Negative Correlations with Positive Lags. The highest negative correlation values with positives lags are in the range $[-0.77, -0.26]$. The highest values are given by APSTUD ($r = -0.77, window = 0, lag = 32$), and TIMOB ($r = -0.55, window = 2, lag = 122$) whereas the remaining projects have correlations with medium effect XD ($r = -0.44, window = 3, lag = 68$), TISTUD ($r = -0.46, window = 3, lag = 89$). The interpretation is that the positive trend in user story quality pays off after 68 (XD), 89 (TISTUD), 122 (TIMOB) business days in the form of a decrease in bug count.

Negative Correlations with Negative Lags. Negative high correlations with negative lags are present in the following projects: XD ($r = -0.33, window =$

$1, lag = -75$), DNN ($r = -0.34, window = 1, lag = -43$), TIMOB ($r = -0.30, window = 0, lag = -85$), TISTUD ($r = -0.47, window = 1, lag = -60$), COMPASS ($r = -0.30, window = 1, lag = -13$), APSTUD ($r = -0.31, window = 2, lag = -18$). A negative correlation with negative lag could indicate that an increase in the number of bugs creates more rework and, thus, leaves less time for conducting proper requirements engineering, which decreases the quality of user stories.

Positive Correlations with Negative Lags. When looking at high positive correlations with negative lags, the results shows correlations in the range $[0.15, 0.27]$: XD ($r = 0.22, window = 3, lag = -76$), TISTUD ($r = 0.24, window = 0, lag = -104$), DNN ($r = 0.15, window = 1, lag = -64$), COMPASS ($r = 0.24, window = 0, lag = -1$), and APSTUD ($r = 0.27, window = 0, lag = -11$). TIMOB does not show a relevant correlation ($r = 0.09, window = 1, lag = -31$). This can be interpreted as follows: an increase in bug count results in an increase in user story quality with a lag of 1 to 104 business days. Possibly, the increase of user story quality was triggered as an attempt to stop a further increase in bug count.

Positive Correlations with Positive Lags. Positive high correlations with positive are present in the following projects: XD ($r = 0.21, window = 2, lag = 47$), DNN ($r = 0.27, window = 0, lag = 19$), TISTUD ($r = 0.21, window = 2, lag = 21$), COMPASS ($r = 0.43, window = 1, lag = 22$), and APSTUD ($r = 0.47, window = 3, lag = 22$). This is difficult to interpret as it seems to suggest that an increase in user story quality yields an increase of bug count after 19 to 47 business days. We can speculate that other factors, e.g., increasing complexity of the system under development, are responsible for the negative effect on bug count. Only additional information could shed light on this.

Rework Count. Figure 4 shows the results of the WTLCC analysis. In the following, we present the relevant correlation values. These results can be interpreted as we presented in full detail for the correlation between user story quality and bug count.

Negative Correlations with Negative Lags. We found correlations in the range $[-0.69, -0.22]$ for the following projects. XD ($r = -0.33, window = 1, lag = -74$), DNN ($r = -0.54, window = 1, lag = -62$), TIMOB ($r = -0.22, window = 3, lag = -141$), TISTUD ($r = -0.40, window = 2, lag = -98$), COMPASS ($r = -0.37, window = 2, lag = -13$), and APSTUD ($r = -0.69, window = 2, lag = -13$).

Negative Correlations with Positive Lags. These type of correlations are present in 4 out of 6 projects, in the range $[-0.40, -0.51]$: XD ($r = -0.50, window = 3, lag = 41$), TIMOB ($r = -0.51, window = 2, lag = 134$), TISTUD ($r = -0.42, window = 3, lag = 96$), COMPASS ($r = -0.40, window = 3, lag = 5$).

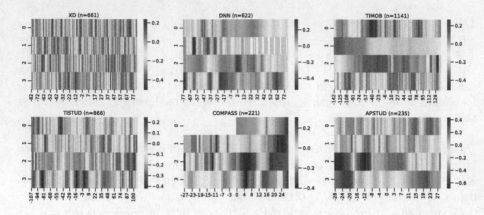

Fig. 4. Heatmaps showing the WTLCC results to compare the quality of user stories with the number of issues with rework done.

Positive Correlations with Negative Lags. We found correlations in the range $[0.22, 0.44]$ for the following projects: XD ($r = 0.22, window = 1, lag = -6$), DNN ($r = 0.33, window = 3, lag = -77$), TIMOB ($r = 0.27, window = 0, lag = -43$), TISTUD ($r = 0.25, window = 3, lag = -85$), and APSTUD ($r = 0.44, window = 2, lag = -27$).

Positive Correlations with Positive Lags. We found correlations in the range $[0.22, 0.31]$ for the following projects: XD ($r = 0.24, window = 0, lag = 72$), DNN ($r = 0.25, window = 2, lag = 2$), TISTUD ($r = 0.22, window = 2, lag = 102$), COMPASS ($r = 0.31, window = 2, lag = 5$), and APSTUD ($r = 0.26, window = 0, lag = 23$).

Delay Count. Figure 5 shows the results of the WTLCC analysis regarding delay count. We present the relevant correlation values. These results can be interpreted as we presented in full detail for the correlation between user story quality and bug count.

Negative Correlations with Negative Lags. We found correlations in the range $[-0.73, -0.16]$ for the following projects. XD ($r = -0.38, window = 2, lag = -76$), DNN ($r = -0.73, window = 1, lag = -28$), TIMOB ($r = -0.16, window = 3, lag = -83$), TISTUD ($r = -0.47, window = 0, lag = -50$), COMPASS ($r = -0.45, window = 3, lag = -10$), and APSTUD ($r = -0.69, window = 3, lag = -6$).

Negative Correlations with Positive Lags. These type of correlations are present in 5 out of 6 projects, in the range $[-0.83, -0.37]$: XD ($r = -0.41, window = 0, lag = 48$), TIMOB ($r = -0.37, window = 2, lag = 100$), TISTUD ($r = -0.49, window = 1, lag = 53$), COMPASS ($r = -0.83, window = 2, lag = 8$), and APSTUD ($r = -0.47, window = 2, lag = 2$).

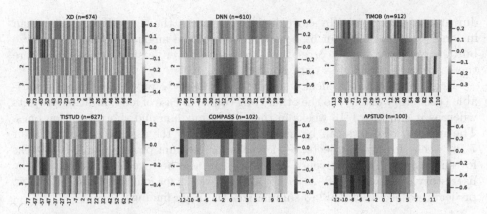

Fig. 5. Heatmaps showing the WTLCC results to compare the quality of user stories with the number of issues with delays.

Positive Correlations with Negative Lags. We found relevant correlations in the range $[0.14, 0.24]$ for the following projects: XD ($r = 0.24, window = 1, lag = -59$), DNN ($r = 0.22, window = 2, lag = -6$), TIMOB ($r = 0.28, window = 0, lag = -31$), TISTUD ($r = 0.24, window = 2, lag = -58$), COMPASS ($r = 0.49, window = 1, lag = -13$), APSTUD ($r = 0.14, window = 1, lag = -7$).

Positive Correlations with Positive Lags. We found correlations in the range $[0.19, 0.51]$ for the following projects: DNN ($r = 0.41, window = 3, lag = 51$), TIMOB ($r = 0.20, window = 3, lag = 94$), TISTUD ($r = 0.19, window = 1, lag = 71$), COMPASS ($r = 0.23, window = 2, lag = 12$), and APSTUD ($r = 0.51, window = 2, lag = 12$). XD has a correlation close to zero ($r = 0.09, window = 2, lag = 65$).

5   Discussion

Regarding the first research question, we observed that the projects exhibit different behaviors in terms of their quality of user stories over time. For example, project XD shows an upward trend in the change of quality. This indicates that the quality was increasing rather than decreasing. On the other hand, COMPASS showed an opposite behavior, where the quality of the user stories decreased as a trend.

The second research question asked about the relationship between User Story quality and the project performance, which is measured by the number of bugs, rework done, and delays. The analysis shows that the projects exhibit an inverse relationship between the quality of user stories and the studied project performance variables. If the quality of user stories increases (decreases), the number of bugs decreases (increase).

Interestingly, our results indicate that the events propagate from one variable to the other at different times (lags), and the lags seem to depend on the whole duration of the project. In short duration projects, the lags where smaller than in long projects. This can be a consequence of the amount of data to analyze but, surprisingly, strong correlations were found even in shorter projects where there are considerable less data points.

Regarding bugs, the effect can take 17–30 weeks to propagate from one variable (user story quality) to the other (bug count) in case of long duration projects whereas it can take 1–13 weeks in the case of medium and short duration ones. The number of delays can be inversely affected by the user story quality after 7–20 weeks for long projects, 8–11 weeks for medium projects, and 1–3 weeks for short ones. The occurrence of rework can also be inversely affected by the user story quality after 18–28, 8–15, and 1–3 weeks for long, medium, and short projects, respectively. Table 3 summarizes the main findings.

Table 3. Summary of results. The cells show the minimum and maximum lags expressed in business weeks (5 business days).

Variable	r	Long duration		Medium duration		Short duration	
		$lag < 0$	$lag > 0$	$lag < 0$	$lag > 0$	$lag < 0$	$lag > 0$
Bugs	$r < 0$	$[-17.0, -5.8]$	$[17.8, 27.8]$	$[-16.0, -8.0]$	$[2.2, 13.6]$	$[-5.6, -2.6]$	$[0.8, 6.4]$
	$r > 0$	$[-22.4, -1.0]$	$[4.2, 9.4]$	$[-15.2, -1.2]$	$[3.8, 14.4]$	$[-2.2, -0.2]$	$[2.4, 4.4]$
Delays	$r < 0$	$[-16.6, -10.0]$	$[7.4, 20.0]$	$[-15.2, -5.6]$	$[8.0, 11.6]$	$[-2.2, -1.2]$	$[0.4, 2.4]$
	$r > 0$	$[-22.8, -3.6]$	$[10.8, 18.8]$	$[-15.2, -1.2]$	$[4.8, 13.0]$	$[-2.6, 0.0]$	$[2.4, 2.4]$
Rework	$r < 0$	$[-28.2, -15.8]$	$[18.6, 28.0]$	$[-14.8, -9.6]$	$[8.2, 15.6]$	$[-4.0, -1.2]$	$[1.0, 3.2]$
	$r > 0$	$[-26.0, -5.4]$	$[20.2, 20.4]$	$[-15.4, -1.2]$	$[0.4, 14.4]$	$[-5.4, -2.2]$	$[1.0, 5.4]$

6   Limitations

The current findings are subject to several limitations that must be considered. It is worth noting that our data-driven approach does not support causal inference and it is mainly based on the discovering of patterns and correlation analysis. Controlled experiments are required to gain insights about causality. Furthermore, the data analysis approach required manual interpretation of visualized results which could have introduced errors. A more systematic approach to interpret the results could improve the accuracy and reliability of the results in further studies. More specifically, the selection of the window size in the WTLCC analyses has a strong influence on the observed results. In our case the window size varied in relation to the overall project duration. Long projects have wide windows and short projects have short windows. The results might change if, for example, uniform window sizes across all analyzed projects are chosen.

Regarding the generalization of the results, they are limited to the data sample. A larger data sample could produce different results, although it is difficult to find open-source projects that use ASD practices and track their process data using publicly available issue trackers. We mitigated this issue by analyzing a heterogeneous set of projects with different characteristics.

Missing values are another threat to validity. The dataset required an extensive amount of data cleaning in order to remove the noise that could have led to misleading conclusions. The projects also show periods of inactivity and we do not know the reasons behind this. To mitigate the impact of these missing data points, we removed the periods of inactivity by manual inspection and we use a linear interpolation method for imputing the remaining missing data points.

Another limitation is introduced by the AQUSA tool. The current development state of the tool is not able to assess the semantics behind the user stories descriptions as it would require expert domain or using advanced artificial intelligence. The AQUSA tool is only able to detect defects related to syntactic and pragmatic aspects of user stories.

In summary, although it is possible to monitor the quality of user stories by using the proposed approach, the process itself is complicated since considerable amount of work has to be done regarding the pre-processing and data cleaning of the data. The visual inspection of the heatmaps can be also prone to errors. Therefore, it can be said that while it is possible to analyze the quality of user stories, more convenient solutions should be developed in order to make the monitoring of user stories simple for development teams.

7   Conclusion

The correlation analysis showed several interesting relationships between the quality of user stories and the project performance measured by the number of bugs, rework, and delays. The results show an inverse relationship between the user story quality and the project performance. When the quality of user stories decreased (increased), the number of bugs increased (decreased) correspondingly. This effect propagates from one variable to another at different lag times, and the lags seem to be related to the whole duration of the project. In particular, long-duration projects exhibit longer propagation time than short-duration projects.

We believe our results shed light on the benefits of writing high-quality user stories when managing requirements in agile software development. In particular, we provide empirical evidence that supports one of the most popular agile practices and the general agile mentors' advice of writing good user stories. Furthermore, this paper integrates previous research into an approach that can be easily extended into a monitoring tool (e.g. a dashboard) that allow developers and stockholders to visualize the overall quality of the written requirements in an aggregated way and set quality standards during the software development.

Acknowledgments. This work was supported by the Estonian Center of Excellence in ICT research (EXCITE), ERF project TK148 IT, and by the team grant PRG 887 of the Estonian Research Council.

Appendix

During the data cleaning phase, we applied the following steps:

1. Removal of empty rows.
2. Removal of special headings in the description of the user story (e.g., "h2. Back story")
3. Removal of hyperlinks to web sites.
4. Removal of mentions to files with extensions such as ".jar".
5. Removal of code examples.
6. Removal of different types of curly brackets combinations.
7. Removal of paths to files.
8. Removal of word whose length is longer than 19 characters. According to [29], words with more than 19 characters are very rare in English (less than 0.1%). In our case, this usually happens when the bod y of a user story describe part of the program code. For example, the string "TriggerSourceOptionsMetadata"
9. Removal of consecutive exclamation marks and the text between them. This notation is commonly used for adding images (e.g., "!GettingStarted.png!")
10. Removal of square brackets and everything between them.
11. Removal of non-ASCII characters.
12. Removal of special characters such as "¡", "¿", "_", and "$".
13. Removal of different kinds of whitespaces (e.g., tabs, " " etc.) and replacing them with a single whitespace.
14. Removal of duplicated User Stories.
15. Removal of upper outliers (abnormally long User Stories). Upper outliers are removed based on the description length using Turkey's fences.
16. Removal of lower outliers (User Stories with less than 3 words). For example, some User Stories consisted of only the description "See: http://...".

References

1. Firesmith, D.: Common requirements problems, their negative consequences, and the industry best practices to help solve them. J. Object Technol. **6**(1), 17–33 (2007)
2. Wohlin, C., et al.: Engineering and Managing Software Requirements. Springer, Heidelberg (2005). https://doi.org/10.1007/3-540-28244-0
3. Cohn, M.: User Stories Applied: For Agile Software Development. Addison-Wesley Professional, Boston (2004)
4. Dingsøyr, T., Nerur, S., Balijepally, V., Moe, N.B.: A decade of agile methodologies. J. Syst. Softw. **85**(6), 1213–1221 (2012)
5. Kassab, M.: The changing landscape of requirements engineering practices over the past decade. In: 2015 IEEE 5th International Workshop on Empirical Requirements Engineering (EmpiRE), pp. 1–8. IEEE (2015)
6. CollabNet VersionOne: 13th Annual State of Agile Report (2018)

7. Wang, X., Zhao, L., Wang, Y., Sun, J.: The role of requirements engineering practices in agile development: an empirical study. In: Zowghi, D., Jin, Z. (eds.) Requirements Engineering. CCIS, vol. 432, pp. 195–209. Springer, Heidelberg (2014). https://doi.org/10.1007/978-3-662-43610-3_15

8. Kassab, M.: An empirical study on the requirements engineering practices for agile software development. In: 2014 40th EUROMICRO Conference on Software Engineering and Advanced Applications, pp. 254–261. IEEE (2014)

9. Lucassen, G., Dalpiaz, F., Werf, J.M.E.M., Brinkkemper, S.: The use and effectiveness of user stories in practice. In: Daneva, M., Pastor, O. (eds.) REFSQ 2016. LNCS, vol. 9619, pp. 205–222. Springer, Cham (2016). https://doi.org/10.1007/978-3-319-30282-9_14

10. Wake, B.: Invest in good stories, and smart tasks (2003)

11. Lucassen, G., Dalpiaz, F., van der Werf, J.M.E., Brinkkemper, S.: Improving agile requirements: the quality user story framework and tool. Requirements Eng. **21**(3), 383–403 (2016)

12. Buglione, L., Abran, A.: Improving the user story agile technique using the invest criteria. In: 2013 Joint Conference of the 23rd International Workshop on Software Measurement and the 8th International Conference on Software Process and Product Measurement, pp. 49–53 (2013)

13. Lai, S.T.: A user story quality measurement model for reducing agile software development risk. Int. J. Softw. Eng. Appl **8**, 75–86 (2017)

14. de Souza, P.L., do Prado, A.F., de Souza, W.L., dos Santos Forghieri Pereira, S.M., Pires, L.F.: Improving agile software development with domain ontologies. In: Latifi, S. (ed.) Information Technology - New Generations. AISC, vol. 738, pp. 267–274. Springer, Cham (2018). https://doi.org/10.1007/978-3-319-77028-4_37

15. Rodríguez-Pérez, G., Robles, G., Serebrenik, A., Zaidman, A., Germán, D.M., Gonzalez-Barahona, J.M.: How bugs are born: a model to identify how bugs are introduced in software components. Empir Software Eng **25**, 1294–1340 (2020)

16. Sedano, T., Ralph, P., Péraire, C.: Software development waste. In: Proceedings of the 39th International Conference on Software Engineering, ICSE 2017, pp. 130–140. IEEE Press (2017)

17. Tamai, T., Kamata, M.I.: Impact of requirements quality on project success or failure. In: Lyytinen, K., Loucopoulos, P., Mylopoulos, J., Robinson, B. (eds.) Design Requirements Engineering: A Ten-Year Perspective. LNBIP, vol. 14, pp. 258–275. Springer, Heidelberg (2009). https://doi.org/10.1007/978-3-540-92966-6_15

18. Jahanshahi, H., Cevik, M., Başar, A.: Predicting the number of reported bugs in a software repository. In: Goutte, C., Zhu, X. (eds.) Canadian AI 2020. LNCS (LNAI), vol. 12109, pp. 309–320. Springer, Cham (2020). https://doi.org/10.1007/978-3-030-47358-7_31

19. Kai, H., Zhengwei, Q., Bo, L.: Network anomaly detection based on statistical approach and time series analysis. In: 2009 International Conference on Advanced Information Networking and Applications Workshops, pp. 205–211 (2009)

20. Herraiz, I., Gonzalez-Barahona, J.M., Robles, G.: Forecasting the number of changes in eclipse using time series analysis. In: 4th International Workshop on Mining Software Repositories, MSR 2007:ICSE Workshops 2007, p. 32 (2007)

21. Choraś, M., Kozik, R., Pawlicki, M., Hołubowicz, W., Franch, X.: Software development metrics prediction using time series methods. In: Saeed, K., Chaki, R., Janev, V. (eds.) CISIM 2019. LNCS, vol. 11703, pp. 311–323. Springer, Cham (2019). https://doi.org/10.1007/978-3-030-28957-7_26

22. Roume, C., Almurad, Z., Scotti, M., Ezzina, S., Blain, H., Delignières, D.: Windowed detrended cross-correlation analysis of synchronization processes. Phys. A **503**, 1131–1150 (2018)
23. Scott, E., Pfahl, D.: Using developers' features to estimate story points. In: Proceedings of the 2018 International Conference on Software and System Process, pp. 106–110 (2018)
24. Scott, E., Charkie, K.N., Pfahl, D.: Productivity, turnover, and team stability of agile software development teams in open-source projects. In: 2020 46th Euromicro Conference on Software Engineering and Advanced Applications (SEAA). IEEE (2020)
25. Porru, S., Murgia, A., Demeyer, S., Marchesi, M., Tonelli, R.: Estimating story points from issue reports. In: Proceedings of the 12th International Conference on Predictive Models and Data Analytics in Software Engineering, pp. 1–10 (2016)
26. Boker, S.M., Rotondo, J.L., Xu, M., King, K.: Windowed cross-correlation and peak picking for the analysis of variability in the association between behavioral time series. Psychol. Meth. **7**(3), 338 (2002)
27. Jammazi, R., Aloui, C.: Environment degradation, economic growth and energy consumption nexus: a wavelet-windowed cross correlation approach. Phys. A **436**, 110–125 (2015)
28. Cohen, J.: A power primer. Psychol. Bull. **112**(1), 155 (1992)
29. Sigurd, B., Eeg-Olofsson, M., Van Weijer, J.: Word length, sentence length and frequency - Zipf revisited. Studia Linguistica **58**(1), 37–52 (2004)

An Approach for Platform-Independent Online Controlled Experimentation

Florian Auer[✉] and Michael Felderer

University of Innsbruck, Innsbruck, Austria
{florian.auer,michael.felderer}@uibk.ac.at

Abstract. Online controlled experimentation is an established technique to assess ideas for software features. Current approaches to conduct experimentation are based on experimentation platforms. However, each experimentation platform has its own explicit properties and implicit assumptions about an experiment. As a result, experiments are incomplete, difficult to repeat, and not comparable across experimentation platforms or platform versions. Our approach separates the experiment definition from the experimentation platform. This makes the experimentation infrastructure-less dependent on the experimentation platform. Requirements on the independent experiment definition are researched and an architecture to implement the approach is proposed. A proof-of-concept demonstrates the feasibility and achieved level of independence from the platform.

Keywords: Online controlled experimentation · Continuous experimentation · Experimentation platform · Experimentation infrastructure

1 Introduction

Online controlled experimentation is an established approach commonly used by organizations to make data-driven decisions about changes in their product. Fabijan et al. conducted in [9] a survey in which they observed that most organizations use in-house built experimentation platforms. Similar in literature, large organizations report of their self-built experimentation platforms, like Microsoft [15] or Google [23]. However, the development of an experimentation platform is a resource-intensive and error-prone project [16]. Thus, many organizations cannot afford to develop a platform. Alternatives are third-party experimentation platforms. But, these platforms do not support all aspects of experimentation [5] and focus more on the technical execution of experiments. For example, not all platforms (proprietary as well as open-source) support the definition of a hypothesis or criteria to automatically shut down an experiment based on business-critical metrics. Thus, it seems that organizations have to choose between high upfront costs of developing an in-house experimentation

© Springer Nature Switzerland AG 2021
D. Winkler et al. (Eds.): SWQD 2021, LNBIP 404, pp. 139–158, 2021.
https://doi.org/10.1007/978-3-030-65854-0_11

platform or to reduce their requirements on experimentation and use a third-party experimentation platform. Moreover, the experiment definitions do not include the implicit assumptions made by the used experimentation platform (e.g. the segmentation algorithm). Hence, the definitions are incomplete and the described experiments are difficult to repeat.

The separation of the experiment definition from the experimentation platform could combine the benefits of both approaches. It would allow organizations to select a cost-effective third-party experimentation platform to execute the experiment while developing independently of it the remaining infrastructure to support the organization's experimentation process. This would, for example, allow developing an infrastructure to assure the quality of the experiments without having to depend on the feature set provided by the experimentation platform.

This research aims to propose an architecture for platform-independent online controlled experimentation by releasing the experiment definition from the experiment platform. As a consequence of the separation, the experiment definition becomes an independent artifact. Moreover, it allows developing experimentation infrastructure independently of the used experimentation platform.

The remainder of this paper is structured as follows. Section 2 provides background information on online controlled experimentation. Section 3 describes the applied research method. Section 4 presents the findings. Then, Sect. 5 presents the architecture, and Sect. 6 the evaluation of it. Section 7 discusses the study. Finally, Sect. 8 concludes the paper.

2   Background

In this section, an overview of the research this paper is based on is given. The overview starts with the general concept of online controlled experimentation. Next, the research on the characteristics of online controlled experiment definitions is outlined, and finally, research on domain-specific language (DSL) to define online controlled experiments is discussed.

2.1   Online Controlled Experimentation

Online controlled experiments are a technique to evaluate software changes based on data [17]. The change could be a novel feature, a performance optimization, modified elements in the user interface, and many more. A version of the software with the change (treatment) is deployed in addition to the unchanged software (control). Thereafter, requests on the software (e.g. user interaction) are split between the two versions (segmentation). In addition to the regular processing of a request, both software versions collect relevant data about the processing and the request. After a predefined duration or number of requests, the collected data (telemetry) is used to calculate metrics. Finally, the telemetry is analyzed, and based on the success criteria that are defined before the execution of the experiment, the experiment is evaluated.

In [2] the authors highlight the technique's potential to improve software quality assurance for modern technologies like machine learning or the internet of things—areas that are challenging for traditional software testing with offline testing techniques.

The experiment lifecycle by Fabijan et al. [8] gives an overview of the activities related to an online controlled experiment (see Fig. 1). First, during the ideation phase, a hypothesis and its implementation are developed. Thereafter, the design of the experiment is specified. This includes amongst others, the user segmentation across the different software versions, and calculations about the size and duration of the experiment. Next, the experiment is executed. Besides the deployment, the instrumentation and monitoring of the deployed software are important. Thereafter, the collected data is analyzed and data-driven arguments for decisions are provided. The last activity is learning, in which the experiment metadata is captured and institutionalized.

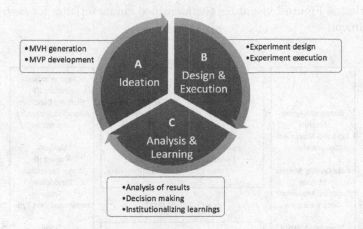

Fig. 1. Experiment lifecycle by Fabijan et al. [8]. It describes the lifecycle of an experiment from its ideation by the generation of a minimal viable hypothesis (MVH) and the development of a minimal viable product (MVP) over the design, execution and analysis to the decision making and institutionalization of the learnings.

A more detailed view of experimentation and its process is given by models for continuous experimentation like the RIGHT model by Fagerholm et al. [13] or the HYPEX (Hypothesis Experiment Data-Driven Development) model by Holmström Olsson and Bosch [20]. There is also research about the required infrastructure [12] and guidelines about experimentation in general [17].

In summary, the process of online controlled experimentation received a lot of attention in research. Process models of continuous experimentation [8,13], experimentation platforms [12] and guidelines [17] for experimentation are researched amongst others.

2.2   Characteristics of Online Controlled Experiments

Although the experimentation process and specifics of it are researched well [1,21], there is little research explicitly on the experimentation definition and its characteristics. Nevertheless, the definition of experiments is fundamental for experimentation. A taxonomy of its characteristics allows experiment owners to choose the necessary characteristics of it for a concrete experiment. Without such an overview, experiment owners are at the risk to miss important characteristics or to define experiments incomplete. Therefore, the authors reviewed in [3] the literature on characteristics of experiment definitions. It revealed 17 properties that were grouped by common themes among the properties.

However, the authors expected that there are additional properties used in practice. Thus, based on the results on the characteristics of experiment definitions, the more detailed study reported in [5] was conducted. The study covers the analysis of existing open-source as well as proprietary experimentation platforms. In [5] the results are combined to one taxonomy of experiment definition characteristics. Figure 2 visualizes the identified characteristics for each phase of an experiment.

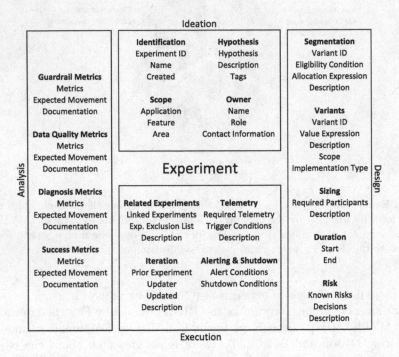

Fig. 2. Experiment definition characteristics taxonomy [5]. It enumerates for every phase of the experimentation lifecycle the characteristics (bold) and their properties (below each characteristic).

To conclude, the authors presented in [5] a taxonomy of the known characteristics and properties used in the definition of online controlled experiments.

However, the application of the taxonomy, or its usefulness to describe experiments was not known.

2.3 Experimentation Definition Language

The taxonomy of experiment definition characteristics [5] represents the characteristics that are used in literature and experimentation platforms. However, it is not fully clear whether this set of characteristics is useful to define concrete experiments. Thus, a DSL was developed in [4] that was built on the taxonomy.

The language allows to describe an experiment with the characteristics of the taxonomy. As the host language, the most commonly used exchange format observed during the analysis of experimentation platforms, JSON (Javascript object notation) was selected. Listing 1.1 provides an experiment defined in the language and shows that the structure follows the taxonomy closely. Each characteristic and its properties can be defined using the JSON syntax.

Listing 1.1. Structure of an experiment written in EDL. It follows closely the structure of the experimentation characteristics taxonomy (see Fig. 2).

```
{
  "Ideation":{
    "Hypothesis":...,
    "Owners":...
  },
  "Design":{
    "Variants":...,
    "Segmentation":...
  },
  "Execution":{
    "AlertingAndShutdown":...
  },
  "Analysis":{
    "SuccessMetrics":...,
    "GuardrailMetrics":...
  }
}
```

A technology acceptance study [4] revealed that the language and the idea of describing an experiment in a structured form, according to the characteristics were accepted by the majority of participants. Moreover, for most participants, the language was considered easy to use. However, the data too showed that there is a relationship between the participant's assessment of the language's ease of use and the participant's background (i.e. business or software engineering).

As a result, the research on a DSL for the definition of an online controlled experiment shows that the developed taxonomy with its characteristics and properties is considered useful. However, the representation of the definition as a DSL hosted in JSON may not be beneficial for all stakeholders.

3 Research Method

This study aims to propose an architecture for platform-independent online controlled experimentation. It is based on the idea of separating the experiment definition from the experimentation platform. Therefore it is necessary to study which elements an experiment definition includes (0.), for what an experiment definition is used during the experiment lifecycle [8] (1.) and what the qualities of an experiment definition are to ensure reliable experimentation (2.). Next (3.), an architecture needs to be designed that meets the identified requirements of (0.) and (1.). Finally, it is necessary to evaluate whether the approach is feasible and beneficial (4.).

The first objective (0.) was mentioned for completeness. It is already researched in [5], in which the authors studied the characteristics specified in an experiment definition. Moreover, in [4] a DSL for an experiment definition was proposed and evaluated. The results are summarized in the Background Section. It follows the objectives researched in this study.

1. *Roles of experiment definitions.* After having studied what characteristics an experiment definition describes, it is necessary to identify the roles that an experiment definition takes in each phase of the experiment lifecycle. The roles describe the applications of the information stored in the experiment definition. Moreover, they make visible the requirements of the experiment definition on the proposed architecture.
2. *Qualities of experiment definitions.* The qualities of an experiment definition are requirements that need to be fulfilled to ensure reliable experimentation. The separation of the experiment definition from the experimentation platform should not impact the quality of an experiment definition or the experiment itself.
3. *Architecture.* An architecture is proposed that separates the experiment definition from the experiment platform. It shows what infrastructure components have to be provided to support all requirements imposed by the identified roles and qualities.
4. *Feasibility.* Finally, the proposed architecture is evaluated about its feasibility and its potential to mitigate the dependency on the experimentation platform. Therefore, a prototypical implementation for an experimental scenario is presented that retains the essence of the problem in an industrial setting. Additionally, the migration to another experimentation platform in the context of the scenario is discussed to evaluate the architecture's independence to the experimentation platform.

The roles and qualities are inferred from the results of the previously conducted literature review [3], observations made during the analysis of open-source as well as proprietary experimentation platforms in [5] and adjustments made during the evaluation. Note that the identified qualities and roles constitute our proposed architecture. However, they are not static nor expected to be complete. Further research on roles and qualities might extend the enumerations about additional roles and qualities.

4 Experiment Definition's Qualities and Roles

In the following the qualities and roles of experiment definitions that were identified from the results of the literature review [3] and observations made during the analysis of experimentation platforms [5] are presented.

4.1 Qualities

Four qualities of experiment definitions were identified.

Knowledge exchange of experimentation results and their implications support the collaborative optimization of systems [19]. Improving the *institutional memory* of experimentation [7] also prevents from accidental repeating already conducted experiments. Therefore, Fabijan et al. [7] suggest building an archive of executed experiments. It should summarize an experiment with metadata like its hypothesis, execution date, and results. A requirement to enable knowledge exchange is that experimentation decisions (like the selection of the learning component [18]) are explicitly documented.

Reproducibility and replicability are two important qualities of an experiment [6]. Reproducibility means that experiments can be independently replicated by another experimenter. Therefore, the context of the experiment and a detailed description of all steps are necessary. Furthermore, Buchert et al. [6] note that "the description of an experiment has to be independent of the infrastructure used". Replicability refers to the act of repeating an experiment under the same conditions, which will lead to the same results.

Traceability. Experiment iterations allow to gradually improve the system under experimentation by iterative adjustments of the parameters in order to maximize a metric of interest [22]. Hence, experiments are commonly part of a series of iterative evolving experiments. Specifications of experiments should therefore highlight the relationship between experiments to improve the traceability.

All of these qualities are supported by the experiment definition language (EDL) [4]. Required characteristics and properties are provided by the language to define reproducible and replicable experiments. Moreover, the language itself is based on the data exchange format JSON which ease the information exchange. Additionally, each characteristic has properties to document the decisions behind the chosen property values. Finally, properties are included that can be used to reference to previous versions of an experiment and document the changes made (see Sect. 2.2).

4.2 Roles

Concerning the roles of an experiment definition, the analysis of the selected papers [3] and observations among experimentation platforms identified that the definition serves various purposes throughout an experiment. Each phase uses the experiment definition in another way (see Fig. 3).

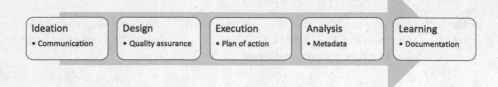

Fig. 3. Main role of the experiment definition in each phase of an experiment. In each phase of the experiment the definition serves another main role.

Communication. A central purpose of the experiment definition is its usage as a communication tool between stakeholders. Online controlled experimentation involves multiple stakeholders that need to exchange information between them. Fagerholm et al. [13] enumerate various stakeholders that are involved in the process of experimentation. The business analysts and product owners that create ideas for experimentation, the data scientist that ensures rigor experimentation, software developers that implement the necessary modifications, quality assurance to verify the software changes, DevOps engineers to deploy the changes, and many more. Although Fig. 3 indicates that communication is used mostly during the ideation of an experiment, activities in all phases can be found that use an experiment definition artifact as a communication tool. For example, the hypothesis made by a business analyst is used by a data scientist to define a fitting segmentation that is used by a DevOps engineer to adapt environment variables. To conclude, all stakeholders use the experiment definition as a tool to manifest and share their decisions on an experiment.

Quality Assurance. The results of an online controlled experiment can have a significant impact on the decisions made by an organization. Hence, it is important to ensure reliable and comprehensible results [19]. Therefore, the quality of experimentation needs to be assured. A structured experiment definition improves the constructive quality of an experiment. It can, for example, limit the number of possible values for a property. In addition, analytical quality approaches can be applied to a definition. Examples are tests to ensure required properties, or sanity-checks on the respective experiment design (e.g. is a user segment assigned to every variant). The definition is used in each phase of an experiment to improve the experiment's quality. For example, in the ideation phase, constructive quality approaches on the definition ensure a solid definition of an experiment idea. During the design phase, analytical quality approaches support the data scientist in the specification of experiment parameters. Moreover, the quality of the experiment execution benefits from a well-structured definition that allows automating previous manual steps. Similarly, the analysis and the learning phase rely on trustworthy information that benefits from a reliable experiment definition. As a result, the experiment definition considerably influences the quality assurance of experimentation throughout each experimentation phase.

Plan of Action. The execution of an experiment requires the accurate execution of a sequence of actions to ensure a trustworthy result. An explicit plan of action that lists all steps of an experiment supports the execution of an experiment. Moreover, it improves the experiment's reproducibility, which is a fundamental quality aspect for experimentation [6]. The experiment definition is implicitly used as a plan of action in the execution phase of an experiment. In this phase, the specified properties are translated into the required actions to set up and execute the experiment. However, other phases use the definition too as the plan of action. For example, during the design phase, development might have to implement changes to the software according to the definition. Similar, analysis, for example, is directed amongst others by the specified metrics and success criteria stated in the definition. To conclude, the experiment definition serves for many activities during an experiment as the plan of action.

Metadata. The definition of an experiment serves as metadata about an experiment [14] during the analysis phase. Data scientists that analyze the collected data are dependent on complete and trustworthy metadata of an experiment to draw conclusions about the collected data. Metadata about an experiment is not only used during the analysis but also, for example, in the ideation phase. Previous experiments could be searched by properties similar to a planned experiment to find relevant experiments and consult their results and learnings [19]. In summary, the experiment definition serves as metadata about an experiment.

Documentation. The prerequisite to draw lessons learned from an experiment is to document it. It is the essential difference between a sequence of independent experiments and continuous experimentation. Although documentation is necessary in each phase of experimentation [14], it is especially relevant for the learning phase. In this phase, the definition serves as a description of the conducted experiment, its idea, the decisions made, and the steps taken. Institutional learning can use this information and draw conclusions from it [10]. For instance, a series of experiments that explore the user habits may reveal that fundamental assumptions about users are no longer true. In addition to learning, documentation can also be useful in other phases of experimentation. For example, during the analysis of an experiment, the documentation of reasons behind decisions made in the design or execution of an experiment gives additional insights into the data. As a result, the experiment definition represents a documentation of an experiment that gives insights into the executed steps and the reasoning behind them.

5 Platform-Independent Experimentation

In this section, the development of the architecture for experimentation platform-independent experimentation is presented. First, the requirements resulting from the roles and qualities identified in the previous sections are discussed. Thereafter, the architecture itself is presented.

5.1 Requirements

The requirements are inferred from the previously identified roles and qualities. Figure 4 visualizes the experimentation lifecycle, the related roles and the requirements on the experiment definition. The definition itself is expected to describe the characteristics of an experiment according to the taxonomy developed in [5]. The qualities are considered in the inferred requirements, which is why they are not explicitly visualized in the figure. In the following, each requirement is discussed in detail.

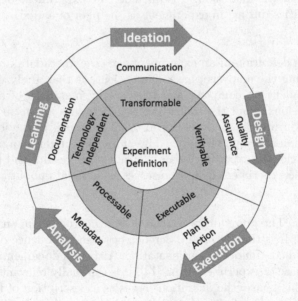

Fig. 4. Roles and requirements of the experimentation definition throughout the experiment lifecycle. The experiment definition (center) is surrounded by its qualities in each phase of the experimentation lifecycle and its main role.

Transformable. The experiment definition not only needs to contain all information relevant for each stakeholder (e.g. hypothesis for the product owner, or segmentation for data scientists) but also be accessible for each stakeholder. The definition needs to be presented in a form that is interpretable and usable for the respective stakeholder and its professional background. The varying fields of expertise of the stakeholders (e.g. business, user experience, development, ...) suggest providing the information in different representations with varying level of detail. For example, developers may prefer a more technical representation (e.g. JavaScript Object Notation), whereas business analysts may prefer a human-readable textual description. Nevertheless, both should work on the same artifact to ensure a single point of truth.

A technology acceptance model study reported in [4] indicates that it is not sufficient to provide one DSL for all possible stakeholders. In the study, a DSL based on the JavaScript Object Notation (JSON) was evaluated. Participants with a strong business background were not as convinced of the language as participants with a technical background.

As a result, the architecture is required to provide information about an experiment in different formats.

Verifiable. Constraints on the structure and the content of the experiment definition are necessary to ensure reliable experimentation. The syntactical verification of the definition is necessary to assure that the properties and values specified in the definition are syntactically correct. Without syntactical valid experiment definitions, the information exchange becomes infeasible. Additional to the syntactical verification, the semantical verification further improves the quality assurance of an experiment. Rules that verify the semantic of a definition complete the verification of an experiment definition. An example of a rule could be that the sum of the user partitioned upon the variants sum up to all users available. Another example could be the enforcement of an organizational rule that for each experiment two owners with emergency contact information need to be defined. Thus, the architecture is required to provide a syntactical verification and the capability to define rules on an experiment definition.

Executable. In the execution phase of the experiment lifecycle, it is required of the experiment definition to provide enough information in a level of detail to infer the plan of action – the steps necessary to execute the experiment. This can include activities like the deployment of a software variant, the collection of data, or the monitoring of shutdown criteria for an experiment (see Fig. 2, Execution). Hence, the definition is required to provide enough information in the necessary level of detail and the architecture is required to interpret the experiment definition and execute the necessary actions to run the experiment.

Processable. The data stored in an experiment definition needs to be in a format that supports the exchange of data between programs. Given that it is the source of information about an experiment, the experiment definition is used by many programs. In order to ease the access of the stored data, the format for the experiment definition artifact should be commonly supported by programs and programming languages.

As a result, the architecture is required to provide the artifact in a commonly supported data exchange format, like XML, JSON, or CSV.

Technology-Independent. The experiment definition should be independent of the concrete technology used to implement the experiment execution, analysis, or archival. The separation between the infrastructure and the experiment definition requires the architecture to provide transformations of the definition of infrastructure specific actions (execution phase) and formats (ideation phase, analysis phase). Nevertheless, the architecture allows creating a robust experiment definition, that is beneficial to documentation, allows interpreting experiment definitions independently of the technology used to execute them, and makes experiments even portable across different experimentation infrastructures.

As a consequence, the architecture is required to define experiments independent of the used technology to conduct the experiment.

5.2 Architecture

The architecture is designed to make a clear distinction between the experiment definition and the experimentation infrastructure (e.g. monitoring service, deployment service). Additionally, it considers all discussed requirements of the experimentation lifecycle on experiment definitions. Note that it is an architecture and not a description of a concrete implementation of a framework. Thus, it focuses on the structure of the system's components it describes. The architecture is visualized in Fig. 5. In the following, the elements of the architecture are described.

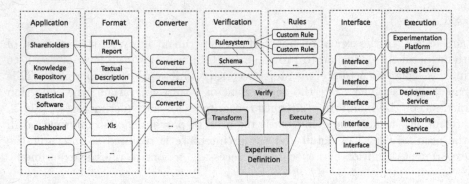

Fig. 5. Architecture for platform-independent online controlled experimentation. The four main elements are the experiment definition, the Transform tool, Verify tool and the Execute tool.

Experiment Definition. In the center of the architecture is the experiment definition artifact. It documents all relevant information of an experiment (e.g. hypothesis, segmentation, or success criteria) according to the taxonomy of experiment characteristics [5]. Therefore, the artifact stores characteristics and their related properties in a systematic way to ensure that the artifact allows systematic access to individual experiment characteristics. Hence, a general data exchange format or a DSL like [4] is suggested as a data format.

Transform. On the left side in Fig. 5, the components that support the transformation of the definition to application-specific formats can be found. The component responsible for this is called *Transform.* It delegates a requested transformation to the appropriate converter. For example, a data scientist may request the metadata of an experiment in the CSV-format for the statistical software R. In this case the Transform component selects among the known converters the appropriate one and executes it. The transformation could also be from an application-specific format to the experiment definition. For a meeting, for instance, the experiment is transformed into an interactive form that allows editing the properties. After the meeting, the form is saved and transformed back to the experiment definition. Note, that the list of formats is exemplary. It depends on the concrete experimentation infrastructure in place and the stakeholders' needs. As a result, the component is extendable by arbitrary converters.

Verify. On top of the experiment definition in Fig. 5 is the *Verify* component. It consists of two subcomponents, namely *Schema* and *Rulesystem.* The *Schema* component verifies the structure of the experiment definition. Most data exchange formats (like XML or JSON) provide a language to describe the structure and verify a document according to it. This technology can be used by the component. The other subcomponent is *Rulesystem.* It is a lightweight, modular system that allows to register custom rules that verify a document syntactically or semantically. A rule, for instance, could be that each experiment has to have a hypothesis following a specific template, like "Based on [qualitative/quantitative] insight, we predict that [change X] will cause [impact Y]" [11]. Rules are a mechanism provided by the architecture to support an automated quality assurance of the experiments. Note that the rules allow to verify an experiment independent of the platform and prior execution of an experiment. Furthermore, they could be used as quality gates that, for example, enforce organizational requirements on an experiment.

Execute. On the right side of the experiment definition in Fig. 5 is the *Execute* component. It is responsible for the interface between the experiment definition and the execution of an experiment. The architecture itself does not include components for the execution or monitoring of an experiment. These are traditional tasks in which experimentation platforms excel [5]. The alternative, to develop custom components that cover tasks like segmentation, is resource-intensive and error-prone as reported in the literature (e.g. [16]). Therefore, the architecture delegates these tasks to individual services or platforms that provide the respective functionality.

6   Evaluation

In this section, a prototypical implementation and an evaluation of the experimentation platform-independent architecture is presented. In the experimental scenario, first, the feasibility of the architecture is evaluated. Second, the claim of platform-independence is validated by changing the experimentation platform and discussing the changes necessary. Finally, the result of the experiment is summarized.

6.1   Scenario

The experimental scenario represents a common infrastructure of an organization developing an Internet service. Thus, common approaches, tools, and methods for the development of an Internet service are assumed. The fictional organization follows the agile development process and uses the Internet service Trello[1] as Kanban board. The developed software is deployed with Docker[2]. Additional assumptions about the scenario are not necessary, given that the experiment focuses on the feasibility and the experimentation platform-independence. Thus, for the scenario, it is not of importance which programming language, libraries, or frameworks are used for the development of the Internet service or possible experiments of it. As experimentation platform the proprietary platform Optimizely[3] was selected.

6.2   System Overview

The implementation consists of three tools, namely `transform`, `verify` and `execute`. For the experiment definition artifact the EDL [4] was selected. It is a DSL based on JSON, which eases the processing of it. As programming language python was used, because of the major ecosystem of libraries and software development kits for third-party applications. An overview of the developed system is visualized in Fig. 6.

The `transform` tool is modular structured and allows adding arbitrary converters in the form of python scripts with the name schema `to-<format>.py` that are located at a specific folder. For the experiment, three converters were implemented that are based on python libraries to convert the information stored in the experiment definition JSON to the respective format.

The `verify` tool is based on two submodules namely `verifySchema` and `verifyRules`. The first, `verifySchema`, provides syntactical verification of the

---

[1] https://trello.com.

[2] https://docker.com.

[3] https://optimizely.com.

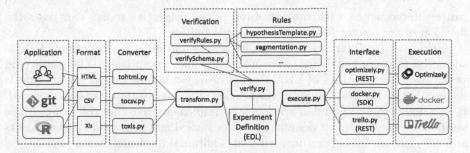

Fig. 6. System overview of the experimental implementation. It demonstrates concrete adaptions of the architecture for the exemplary scenario.

experiment definition. Therefore, the JSON schema definition of the EDL is used to automatically verify the syntax of the definition artifact. The second submodule, `verifyRules` verifies the artifact semantically by executing custom rules against the experiment definition. Rules are python scripts that are located at a specific folder. They can be specific to the project (e.g. 20% is the minimum allocation of users for the unmodified variant) or organization (e.g. two experimentation owners at least).

The `execute` tool is similar implemented as the `transform` tool. It allows adding arbitrary scripts that interpret the experiment definition and execute the related interface calls. In the experimental scenario, three interfaces were considered. An interface to the experimentation platform Optimizely to deploy the experiment on the experimentation platform, another to docker to deploy the software version under experimentation and the third to Trello to create a task for Operations to monitor the experiment. All three of them are built on SDKs or REST APIs that are provided by the tools. The prototypical implementation is available at GitHub[4].

6.3   Feasibility

The feasibility is evaluated by the implementation of the described experimental scenario and the researchers' observations doing so. Therefore, in the following, each components' development is discussed.

Initially, the format and language of the experiment definition artifact had to be selected. A common data exchange format is beneficial, given that the information stored in the artifact needs to be processed by multiple programs. The EDL [4] was selected because it is based on JSON and provides a Schema with all necessary characteristics and properties of an experiment. Given that the verification and interpretation of the artifact are delegated to the `verify` and `execute` tool, a generic experiment definition language like EDL can be used without modifications. Project-specific interpretations or verification rules

---

[4] https://github.com/auerflorian/platform-independent-experimentation-prototype.

can be implemented with the extension of the respective tools. This eases the decision of the format for the experiment definition.

Next, the tool `verify` that verifies the definition was implemented. It is supposed to verify the definition syntactically and semantically. The syntactical verification is in the case of EDL already provided by the JSON Schema that is defined for it. For the semantic verification, the rule system was implemented. It is a lightweight, modular approach to implement reusable rules. Thus, the verification of experiment definitions can be reused and improved across projects and for different infrastructures without additional implementation effort.

The `transform` tool has a modular architecture and calls the appropriate converter provided as a script within a specific folder. For the implementation of the specific converters, the selected format of the experiment definition artifact was beneficial. JSON stores data objects and thus provides a rich structure of the data, which is used by the EDL to provide the characteristics and properties of an experiment in a structure of hierarchical objects. The additional information by the hierarchy of the individual properties ease the conversion. For example, the hierarchy of the properties could be translated to headings for a report in an HTML report.

Finally, the `execute` tool that redirects calls to the appropriate interface was implemented. For the experimental scenario, an interface to Optimizely, docker, and Trello was implemented. All three systems provide REST APIs or SDKs. Thus, the interface's main complexity was in the interpretation of the experiment definition and translation of it into system-specific function calls. For example, for the experimentation platform Optimizely, the initial implementation created an experiment on the platform according to the experiment definition. In the next iteration, the interface, first verified that there is not already an experiment wit the same ID on the platform. A future iteration could consider to update the experiment specification according to the experiment definition. This demonstrates that the implementation of an interface to an experimentation platform is not a trivial task, if all possible states of the experiment definition and the experimentation platform have to be considered. Note, however, that the proposed architecture does not specify where in the process of experimentation or of the software development process the tools are executed. Thus, with additional call arguments and the integration of the tools at the right places within the development process the complexity of the interfaces could be reduced. Nevertheless, the integration of third-party tools through interfaces introduced the most complexity in the implementation of the proposed architecture.

6.4   Platform-Independence

The platform-independency of the proposed architecture is evaluated with a theoretical modification to the experimental scenario. Therefore, the following addition to the scenario description is assumed:

After a year of experimentation, the organization reevaluates the infrastructure used to identify possible optimizations. The analysis of the infrastructure components revealed that there is another more cost-effective experimentation platform available. Thus, the experimentation platform needs to be changed.

This scenario can lead to considerable migration costs without the application of the proposed platform-independent architecture. All experiment definitions are stored implicitly within the platform. Moreover, the process of experimentation is coupled to the platform and its implicit experimentation lifecycle. Thus, with the change of the platform not only the existing knowledge base of experiments may be lost, but also the process of experimentation, that requires an expensive adaptation of the process to the new platform. Additionally, verification rules that were implicitly in the previous experimentation platform may no longer exist in the new platform or may have changed. To summarize, the migration to another experimentation platform has a considerable impact on the whole experimentation process.

In contrast, with a platform-independent architecture, the migration is reduced to a new implementation of an experiment platform interface. Metadata about existing experiments is not affected and would still be "executable". Moreover, the process of experimentation is not affected. Verification, for example, follows the same organization-defined rules as with the previous experimentation platform.

Note, that in both cases the migration to another experimentation platform may require changes in the software, deployment, or infrastructure. For instance, the interface for the platform has to be implemented and the related code sections within the software that request the experimentation platform to decide which variant to show, have to be adapted. Nevertheless, neither the experiment definition nor the generators or the verification should be affected by the migration.

6.5   Experimental Result

The experimental scenario of an organization developing an Internet service was presented. An implementation of the proposed architecture demonstrated the feasibility of it. The description of the development indicates the implementation effort of its components and may allow reasoning about the possible return of investment when compared, for example, to the outlined benefits in the case of a migration to another experimentation platform.

Finally, the scenario was adapted to portrait the possible impacts of a migration. Thereby, it was argued that the proposed architecture is experimentation platform-independent by considering the changes that are necessary in the case of a migration to another experimentation platform.

7   Discussion

The study identified the roles of an experiment definition throughout the experimentation lifecycle. It shows that in each phase of the lifecycle, the definition of an experiment plays an important role. Moreover, the described qualities and requirements on the experiment definition make the strong impact of the definitions on the success of an experiment visible. For example, its appropriateness as a tool for communication in the ideation phase for each shareholder, the precise representation of the experiment for verification, or its availability in a processable form for the analysis of the collected data.

In addition, the study indicated how dependent the experimentation process is on the experimentation platform that commonly provides the (implicit) experiment definition. Furthermore, the implicit experiment definition of third party experimentation platforms introduces a risk of vendor lock-in. A data-exchange format for experiment definitions does not exist. Thus all metadata about experiments is platform-specific and may not always be exportable. Thus, it is not surprising that most organizations do not use third party experimentation platforms, as the survey [9] among practitioners indicates. However, the development of a self-built experimentation platform is not feasible for every organization. The high upfront cost of time and resources to develop a reliable experimentation platform [16] are not manageable for every organization.

The proposed experimentation platform-independent architecture mitigates the impact of a platform on the experimentation lifecycle. Despite the use of a third-party experimentation platform, the organization can define and adjust its experimentation lifecycle. Moreover, the migration to another experimentation platform becomes feasible as discussed in the experimental scenario of a migration.

Limitations. Even though possible threats to validity were considered during the design and execution of the study, the findings of this experiment have to be interpreted within their limitations. The main limitation of the study is the evaluation of the proposed architecture. Although the technical feasibility was evaluated by a proof-of-concept implementation, the organizational feasibility of the approach cannot be demonstrated with this method. Thus, the evaluation does not show whether the approach would also be feasible to be followed by a team. However, the construction of the architecture that is based on the requirements on the experiment definition is expected to have guided the development of the architecture to be also organizational feasible. The second point of evaluation was the platform-independence. This was evaluated by the discussion of the impacts of a migration to another experimentation platform to stress the dependency of the architecture to the experimentation platform. Even though the evaluation was only done by the discussion of the theoretical implications, the impacts are arguable sufficiently predictable on the architecture to use this evaluation technique.

8   Conclusions

Organizations that use third-party experimentation platforms are in the risk of a vendor lock-in. The implicit experimentation lifecycle enforced by the platform and the predefined definition of an experiment requires the organization to adapt its experimentation process to the platform. To mitigate this risk, an experimentation platform-independent architecture is proposed.

The proposed architecture separates the experiment definition from the experimentation platform. Therefore, the qualities and roles of experiment definitions were studied to develop an architecture that separates the definition from the platform without mitigating a role or a quality of the definition. The conducted evaluation suggest that the architecture is feasible and mitigates the impact of the experimentation platform on experimentation.

Interesting future research directions are the conduction of a case study to observe the architecture in an industrial setting. This could further improve the evaluation of the architecture and show the benefits as well as disadvantages of the approach.

References

1. Auer, F., Felderer, M.: Current state of research on continuous experimentation: a systematic mapping study. In: 2018 44th Euromicro Conference on Software Engineering and Advanced Applications (SEAA). IEEE (2018)
2. Auer, F., Felderer, M.: Shifting quality assurance of machine learning algorithms to live systems. In: Software Engineering und Software Management 2018 (2018)
3. Auer, F., Felderer, M.: Characteristics of an online controlled experiment: preliminary results of a literature review. arXiv preprint arXiv:1912.01383 (2019)
4. Auer, F., Felderer, M.: Evaluating the usefulness and ease of use of an experimentation definition language. In: 2020 32th International Conference on Software Engineering and Knowledge Engineering. KSI Research Inc. and Knowledge Systems Institute Graduate School (2020)
5. Auer, F., Lee, C.S., Felderer, M.: Continuous experiment definition characteristics. In: 2020 46th Euromicro Conference on Software Engineering and Advanced Applications (SEAA). IEEE (2020)
6. Buchert, T., Ruiz, C., Nussbaum, L., Richard, O.: A survey of general-purpose experiment management tools for distributed systems. Fut. Gener. Comput. Syst. **45**, 1–12 (2015). https://doi.org/10.1016/j.future.2014.10.007
7. Fabijan, A., Dmitriev, P., Olsson, H.H., Bosch, J.: The evolution of continuous experimentation in software product development: from data to a data-driven organization at scale. In: 2017 IEEE/ACM 39th International Conference on Software Engineering (ICSE). IEEE (2017). https://doi.org/10.1109/icse.2017.76
8. Fabijan, A., Dmitriev, P., Olsson, H.H., Bosch, J.: The online controlled experiment lifecycle. IEEE Softw. **37**, 60–67 (2018)
9. Fabijan, A., Dmitriev, P., Olsson, H.H., Bosch, J.: Online controlled experimentation at scale: an empirical survey on the current state of a/b testing. In: 2018 44th Euromicro Conference on Software Engineering and Advanced Applications (SEAA), pp. 68–72. IEEE (2018)
10. Fabijan, A., Dmitriev, P., Olsson, H.H., Bosch, J., Vermeer, L., Lewis, D.: Three key checklists and remedies for trustworthy analysis of online controlled experiments at scale. In: 2019 IEEE/ACM 41st International Conference on Software Engineering: Software Engineering in Practice (ICSE-SEIP), pp. 1–10. IEEE (2019)

11. Fabijan, A., Dmitriev, P., Olsson, H.H., Bosch, J., Vermeer, L., Lewis, D.: Three key checklists and remedies for trustworthy analysis of online controlled experiments at scale. In: 2019 IEEE/ACM 41st International Conference on Software Engineering: Software Engineering in Practice (ICSE-SEIP). IEEE (2019). https://doi.org/10.1109/icse-seip.2019.00009

12. Fagerholm, F., Guinea, A.S., Mäenpää, H., Münch, J.: Building blocks for continuous experimentation. In: Proceedings of the 1st International Workshop on Rapid Continuous Software Engineering, pp. 26–35 (2014)

13. Fagerholm, F., Guinea, A.S., Mäenpää, H., Münch, J.: The right model for continuous experimentation. J. Syst. Softw. **123**, 292–305 (2017)

14. Gupta, S., Ulanova, L., Bhardwaj, S., Dmitriev, P., Raff, P., Fabijan, A.: The anatomy of a large-scale experimentation platform. In: 2018 IEEE International Conference on Software Architecture (ICSA), pp. 1–109. IEEE (2018)

15. Kevic, K., Murphy, B., Williams, L., Beckmann, J.: Characterizing experimentation in continuous deployment: a case study on Bing. In: 2017 IEEE/ACM 39th International Conference on Software Engineering: Software Engineering in Practice Track (ICSE-SEIP), pp. 123–132. IEEE (2017)

16. Kohavi, R., Deng, A., Frasca, B., Longbotham, R., Walker, T., Xu, Y.: Trustworthy online controlled experiments: five puzzling outcomes explained. In: Proceedings of the 18th ACM SIGKDD International Conference on Knowledge Discovery and Data Mining, pp. 786–794 (2012)

17. Kohavi, R., Longbotham, R., Sommerfield, D., Henne, R.M.: Controlled experiments on the web: survey and practical guide. Data Min. Knowl. Discov. **18**(1), 140–181 (2008). https://doi.org/10.1007/s10618-008-0114-1

18. Mattos, D.I., Bosch, J., Holmström Olsson, H.: More for less: automated experimentation in software-intensive systems. In: Felderer, M., Méndez Fernández, D., Turhan, B., Kalinowski, M., Sarro, F., Winkler, D. (eds.) PROFES 2017. LNCS, vol. 10611, pp. 146–161. Springer, Cham (2017). https://doi.org/10.1007/978-3-319-69926-4_12

19. Issa Mattos, D., Dmitriev, P., Fabijan, A., Bosch, J., Holmström Olsson, H.: An activity and metric model for online controlled experiments. In: Kuhrmann, M., et al. (eds.) PROFES 2018. LNCS, vol. 11271, pp. 182–198. Springer, Cham (2018). https://doi.org/10.1007/978-3-030-03673-7_14

20. Olsson, H.H., Bosch, J.: From opinions to data-driven software R&D: a multicase study on how to close the open loop problem. In: 2014 40th EUROMICRO Conference on Software Engineering and Advanced Applications, pp. 9–16. IEEE (August 2014). https://doi.org/10.1109/seaa.2014.75

21. Ros, R., Runeson, P.: Continuous experimentation and A/B testing: a mapping study. In: Proceedings of the 4th International Workshop on Rapid Continuous Software Engineering (RCoSE), pp. 35–41. ACM (2018). https://doi.org/10.1145/3194760.3194766

22. Tamburrelli, G., Margara, A.: Towards automated a/b testing. In: Le Goues, C., Yoo, S. (eds.) SSBSE 2014. LNCS, vol. 8636, pp. 184–198. Springer, Cham (2014). https://doi.org/10.1007/978-3-319-09940-8_13

23. Tang, D., Agarwal, A., O'Brien, D., Meyer, M.: Overlapping experiment infrastructure: more, better, faster experimentation. In: Proceedings of the 16th ACM SIGKDD International Conference on Knowledge Discovery and Data Mining, pp. 17–26 (2010)

Author Index

Printed in the United States
By Bookmasters